Glorified Fasting

By Franklin Hall

ISBN: 978-1-63923-580-3

Printed: January 2023

Published and Distributed By:
Lushena Books
607 Country Club Drive, Unit E
Bensenville, IL 60106
www.lushenabks.com

ISBN: 978-1-63923-580-3

PART I

FASTING POWER

I will praise thee; for I am fearfully and wonderfully made: marvelous are the works; and thy soul knoweth right well. Psalm 139:14.

Most Christian people are happy to receive teaching on the subject of the consecration fast. More than ninety-five percent of all questions asked concerning the subject pertain to the natural. Before we can properly enter a prophet's length fast, one should familiarize himself with the subject in order to be free from the bugaboos that Satan may hold over one and also to be able to obtain everything out of the fast that is for us.

WITNESSING SIDELIGHT FROM AUTHOR

The author practices his own teachings. When a boy in school he was ill most of the time. His grades were failing. Headaches, colds, poor memory and many other negative things were experienced. He would grab for anything he could find along the lines of health and study it. Although his uncle, Dr. Wm. Hall, was a family physician, the medicine, the prescriptions did but little good. Finally he began to acquire knowledge about fasting. With the Bible he learned more about this subject. As he began to fast with his prayer life, he found Isaiah 58:8 very true. ". . .

LIGHT shall BREAK FORTH AS THE MORNING, AND THINE HEALTH SHALL SPRING FORTH SPEEDILY: AND THY RIGHTEOUSNESS SHALL GO BEFORE THEE; **the glory of the Lord shall be thy reward.**" Fasting surely brings about speedy health.

Soon Brother Hall saw the revelation of food addiction bondage. An addiction bondage that many fine people including Christians were seldom aware of. Immediately Brother Hall gave up entirely and completely his morning breakfast. From a lad in school to this day, Brother Hall has not eaten breakfast.

RESULTS:

From that day to this the author has not had a single headache. Grades were much better in school. By living the fasted life, by fasting regularly, Brother Hall now has better health than he had more than fifty years ago. His hair has not thinned. In fact he has a thicker head of hair than he had upon his head 50 years ago. Many great and wonderful revelations come to him, including the great truth of the FULLNESS OF THE BAPTISM OF HOLY GHOST AND FIRE UPON BODIES THAT BRINGS ABOUT LIKEWISE THE FUNDAMENTAL BODYFELT SALVATION. Our bodies may also become saved. Saved from all harm, all sickness, accidents and from all dangerous things.

It was through much fastings that this, one of the greatest revelations has come about. This new (old Bible) truth is spreading everywhere and it is growing because it is a Kingdom of Heaven truth that will bring about the coming of Jesus.

There was a fencing master who never lost a duel. His movements were so swift, his aim so true, and his skill so astounding, that he was a source of amazement to all who beheld him in action. However, his secret was simple. Before any duel or engagement was entered into he, of course, would practice faithfully for hours. In addition, he would fast from seven to ten days.

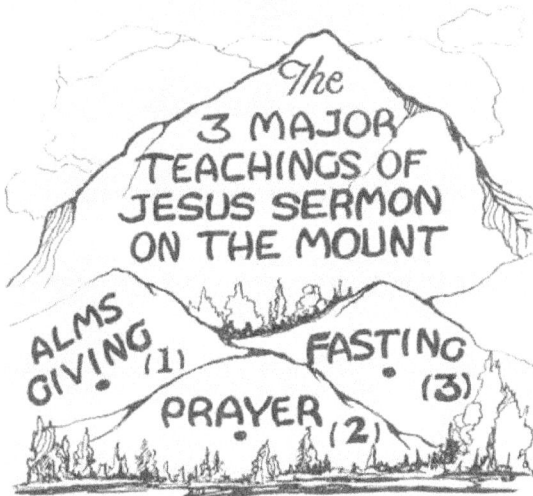

The
3 MAJOR
TEACHINGS OF
JESUS SERMON
ON THE MOUNT

ALMS GIVING (1)

PRAYER (2)

FASTING (3)

The Three Great
FUNDAMENTALS
OF CHRIST ~

1. MATT. 6. 1-4
2. "   6.5-15
3. "   6.16-18

The world has recently witnessed a graphic demonstration of the effect of fasting on the hunger-strikers. If all others had deserted their cause, the hunger-strikers who survived would still cherish the ideals they were willing to die for. No cause will ever be deserted whose champions have fasted for it.

This points to fasting as a panacea against all the evils of backsliding, and the indifference and superficiality which, like a religious hook-worm, saps the energies of the church.

Mahatma Gandhi[1], along with his people, has known more than his share of persecution, trials and tribulations. When a crisis is at hand, he invariably goes on a fast, and, nearly always, something happens to ease the situation. He is no longer held in contempt for his many fastings. His people revere him as a holy man, and even government circles pay him honor and respect. Gandhi has trouble—he fasts and has victory even though his religion is contrary to ours.

A business man has financial reverses and is on the verge of bankruptcy. In his despair, he forgets everything, even food. With many days fasting, many times he will find a way out. No doubt, the Lord is mercifully and tenderly watching over this man, even though he may be unaware of the fact. We are told the Lord allows it to rain on the just and the unjust alike.

A football player leaves off a meal or two before a game and plays more efficiently.

Many persons, including singers, actors, professional people and factory workers, have fasted, and have known either a large or small degree of success in connection with the object they fasted for. No doubt, it developed faith in what they were doing. "There is no habit or weakness that can survive a siege of prayer and fasting—prayer alone is not half the battle," states E. E. Purinton, in his book, 'Philosophy of Fasting." However fasting is not a cure-all for moral, physical and religious problems. Jesus is the answer to this.

It would seem like magic the way fasting works in the natural. If fasting has power to help natural people in their work and with their problems, how much more effectively could this powerful force be utilized for the glory of Jesus.

Moses undertook two forty-day fasts, and there was revealed to him the application of the law to all phases of life. Ex. 24:18; 34:27,28.

The Psalms are largely the product of fasting and prayer.

The book of Daniel, the first book of the Revelation, is another fasting book, given because Daniel sought the Lord in much fasting and prayer. After he fasted twenty-one days, he received the revelation of "what shall befall thy people in the latter days." Dan. 10:2.

Daniel was no more entitled to this revelation than any other man, but since he had sought it by fasting and prayer, it was given him.

The Revelation of Jesus Christ (Rev. 1:1) was given to John on the bare and rugged Isle of Patmos, where he was placed to starve to death. John, being a very spiritual person, immediately converted his intended starvation into one of the greatest consecration fasts. God's people will never know famines in the real sense of the word if they would follow the examples of Elijah, John and other Holy men who converted famines into fastings. Therefore, we have the product of fasting and prayer. Revelation of this kind nearly always came to a prophet on an empty stomach. A product can be traced to its cause. We find in Bible days, and in our own time, when a person goes into a prophet's-length fast, revelation is one of the most wonderful results. If I have ice, the cause is water exposed to such a low temperature that it freezes. The result is ice.

Elijah, after a fast of forty days, received the revelation of the nature and manifestation of God. It was also revealed to him who was to succeed him as prophet, and who were to be the successors of the kings of Israel and of Syria.

Ezra proclaimed a fast for his companions at the river of Ahava, when he was seeking God's help and guidance in the work they were about to undertake. Ezra 8:21-23.

Esther, when about to intercede with Ahasuerus in behalf of the Jews, commanded the Jews of Shushan to fast for three days; this was for the purpose of obtaining wisdom as well as divine favor. Esther 4:16.

To Anna, the prophetess, who "served God with fastings and prayer night and day," it was revealed that the infant being presented was the Messiah. Luke 2:36. Fasting did not impair her health. On the contrary, her great age was given to prove fasting beneficial.

On the fourth day of a fast, it was revealed to Cornelius where he would find Peter, through whom he would receive the Gospel. Acts 10:30. Peter had evidently been fasting, too, because he was very hungry.

After Saul fasted and prayed for three days, it was revealed to him that Ananias would come and restore his sight, and likewise reveal "what he must do." Acts 9:7.

7

After Paul fasted thirteen days, he received the revelation that he would not perish, but would be brought before Caesar, and that his prayers would be heard in behalf of his shipmates. Acts 27:21-33.

Many founders of religious systems fasted for long periods in caves or wilderness, and whatever truth their systems contain beyond contemporary knowledge, is the product of their prayer and fasting.

Buddha Sakia fasted 47 days before the revelation came. Mahomet fasted long periods while continually calling on God for revelation.

Dr. Tanner, fasted over forty days on three different occasions, and had spiritual revelation, seeing the unspeakable glories of the great Beyond. After the last fast, his gray hair began turning black.

Sadhu Sundar Singh, the St. Paul of India and Tibet, fasted forty days, and obtained such a revelation of the presence and nearness of God that it has been a powerful factor in his success as an evangelist.

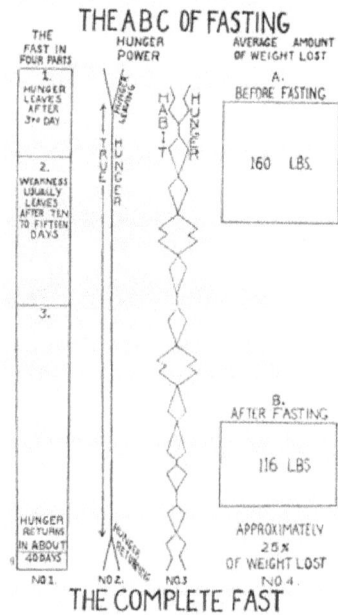

THE ABC OF FASTING

THE FAST IN FOUR PARTS	HUNGER POWER	AVERAGE AMOUNT OF WEIGHT LOST
1. HUNGER LEAVES AFTER 3rd DAY		A. BEFORE FASTING
2. WEAKNESS USUALLY LEAVES AFTER TEN TO FIFTEEN DAYS		160 LBS.
3.		
		B. AFTER FASTING
		116 LBS.
HUNGER RETURNS IN ABOUT 40 DAYS		APPROXIMATELY 25% OF WEIGHT LOST
NO.1	NO.2 NO.3	NO.4

THE COMPLETE FAST

Jesus Christ fasted forty days and nights . . . healing all manner of disease among the people. And His fame went throughout." Matt. 4:23,24. He began His ministry, His manifestation of Sonship, and started performing miracles after His long FAST.

In 1920, an ignorant Denver shoemaker named Francis Schlatter, suddenly became transformed into a miracle-worker. After fasting for forty days, this Catholic shoemaker received the gift of healing and began praying for people everywhere. Many very notable healings occurred.

8

Brother William Branham had received the gift of divine healing about the same time the author wrote "Atomic Power With God." This was during the period men and women were fasting twenty-one to forty days for the power to be restored in the church of Jesus Christ. Brother Branham told me, "when I live the fasted life, the gift is in full operation. An angel appeared before me and said, 'nothing will stand in my way, even cancers will be removed.' There has been nothing that has failed to respond to me when I wait on the Lord and live the fasted life." The author was with Brother Branham in a recent meeting and every sick and diseased person that was prayed for was healed, including a man brought in on a stretcher whose death was expected at any moment, but who arose, instantly healed, and walked away. Several deaf and dumb mutes were immediately healed, as were cross-eyes, cancer cases, and folk in wheel chairs who rose up and walked home.

Brother Branham informed me he had his greatest meetings where the author has gotten many folk to fast, and has placed much fasting literature. Where fasting chains were organized, the healing power was manifested in an unusual manner. This was true in Canada, St. Louis, Portland and Salem, Oregon, where the Governor and other State officials attended. Brother Branham has informed the author his gift is in answer to the many fastings and prayers of the Lord's people. His work is interdenominational, but he holds Baptist credentials.

Brother William Hooley, of Winnipeg, Canada, also fasted, in travail, twenty-one and forty days for Brother Branham's gift and success.

More and more people will receive this spiritual power as soon as they follow through the complete teachings of Jesus. Are you doing your part?

The Church becomes Powerless Without these FIRM FOUNDATIONS

GIVING PRAYER FASTING

FASTING BRINGS THE CLOUD

OF FIRE INTO VISIBILITY

Holy Ghost and Fire Comes upon Body—

No More Cold Feet

Dear Brother and Sister Hall:

I am sending in and offering to help in this wonderful Bodyfelt as well as Heartfelt and fasting and prayer ministry.

I thank the Lord for your fasting and prayers for me. After I wrote in to you for this request, I also felt led to go on a fast. As I fasted and broke the fast I began feeling so much better and so wonderful. I had very little weakness on the fast. I was not very hungry.

On a longer fast I was studying and praying, suddenly a ball of fire appeared at the window of my room. It seemed to be alive with wings of healings. Long objects came forth from the Cloud of fire. This was the first time in my life that I ever saw the Cloven Tongues like Fire objects. A little later on I again saw these wings come out of the Cloud of Fire. It only happened when I was fasting. When on these fasts I see these glorious objects. It just seems like a little bit of heaven comes down upon me and to me. Another time it appeared like white pearls that glistened with the glory of the Lord.

If it is this wonderful now, leaving me covered with some of the Holy Ghost healing Fire upon my body, what will it be like when I become completely covered with the Holy Ghost Substance?

First Winter To Have My Feet Good and Warm

By these fasts I just seem to feel the power of God come upon my body. This wonderful Light and Heat Substance is getting stronger upon my body so that I am experiencing the Bodyfelt Salvation more and more. I am so thankful that I have received the depth of it sufficiently upon my feet that I do not have cold feet anymore. I have always had cold feet. This winter is the first winter not to have cold feet. The Holy Ghost Healing Fire keeps them warm.

Sister Gertrude Farmer, Webster, Mass.

THE POWER THAT FOOD PLAYS UPON THE MENTAL FACULTIES.

This diagram may help to enable one to understand why it is difficult to get into the proper frame of mind, and become loosened from food bondage for a season to begin a consecrated fast to the glory and edification of Jesus Christ, and give the tabernacle of the Holy Spirit a good old-fashion cleaning.

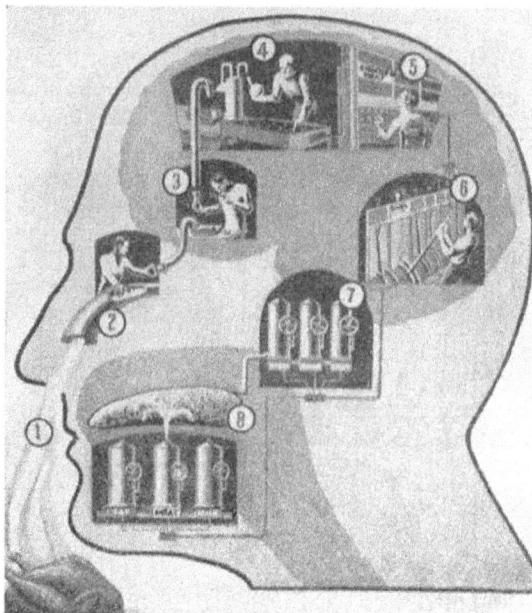

(1) The food, or roast odor, ascends the nose and stimulates the olfactory cells of the nasal mucosa (2); this stimulus is transmitted to the olfactory center In the brain (3). The memory center (4) determines that the odor is that of a roast foul, and orders the gland center (5) to switch on the salivary gland. The order is transmitted to the switchboard (6), where one of the salivary glands (7 and 8) is turned on. From here on we enjoy eating food.

ILLUSTRATING WHY FASTING IS
MORE POWERFUL THAN PRAYER ALONE

1. CARNAL ZONE

2. PLEASURE ZONE

PLEASURE STILL ENJOYED WHILE PRAYING

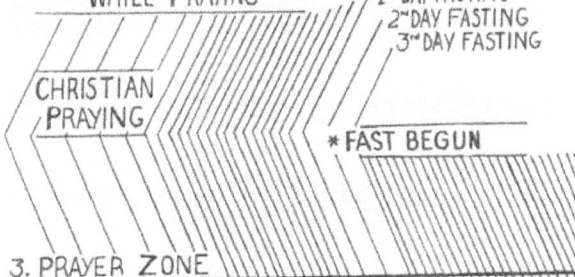

1ˢᵗ DAY FASTING
2ⁿᵈ DAY FASTING
3ʳᵈ DAY FASTING

CHRISTIAN PRAYING

* FAST BEGUN

3. PRAYER ZONE

4. MOURNING [CONSECRATED] FASTING ZONE   FASTING IS AN ANTI-PLEASURE

* WHEN FASTING ONE HAS NO CAPACITY
FOR PLEASURE (ZONE 2) LET ALONE CARNALITY

THIS IS TYPICAL OF THE CONSECRATION FAST. WHEN THE FAST IS NOT IN DEEP CONSECRATION, SOMETIMES PLEASURE CAN BE FOUND. Isa. 58:3.

1. Gandhi, age 78, was assassinated January 30, 1948. His physicians stated that he was in better health at this time than the average man of that age.

PART II

HOW TO BEGIN A FAST

It is very easy to start a fast of any length. If the work is not too strenuous and one cannot very well get off from one's job, the candidate can begin fasting and continue working. Since our main object is to seek Jesus in prayer and the humiliation of the flesh through fasting, one's prayer life will not be so concentrated when working, however, Jesus promises us a reward when we fast (separate from prayer, mind you) in Matt. 6:18, for proper fasting. Rather than not fast at all and work, one could begin a fast and see how long he could keep both up. If it became too difficult to fast and work, one could of course, break the fast properly, at any time. To obtain the best from the fast, we should do much praying—and praying will be work. It is also MUCH EASIER TO FAST while active. Walking and praying is one of the best exercises for the faster. Hunger will also return more quickly when exercising. Prayer can be made a fine spiritual and physical exercise.

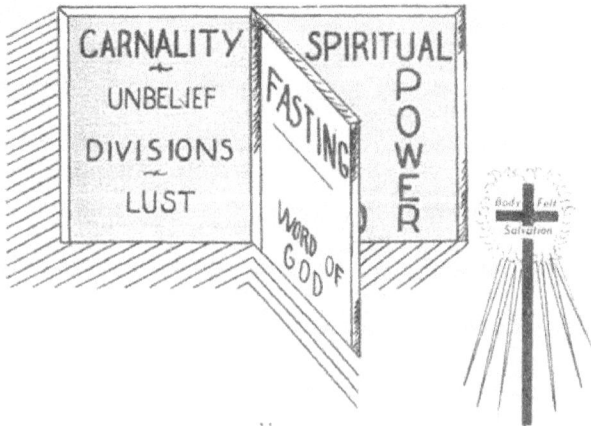

THE SAME DOOR THAT CLOSES CARNALITY OPENS UP THE **SPIRITUAL**

CARNALITY
UNBELIEF
DIVISIONS
LUST

FASTING
WORD OF GOD

SPIRITUAL
POWER

Body Felt
Salvation

— 11 —

14

One can begin fasting by abstaining from the next meal and continue his fast as long as it will glorify Jesus. The depression, remorse, anti-pleasure and other strange and oppressed feelings from Satan, are no excuse to break a fast prematurely. Most of these feelings are the fighting and gaining of victorious ground into faith that we so greatly need. The victory usually comes after the fast.

WHEN LIVING BY BREAD ALONE

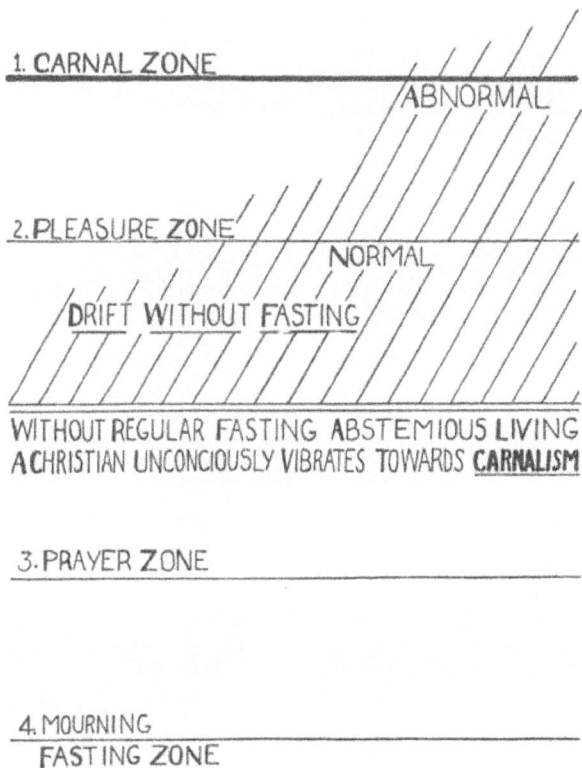

1. CARNAL ZONE

ABNORMAL

2. PLEASURE ZONE

NORMAL

DRIFT WITHOUT FASTING

WITHOUT REGULAR FASTING ABSTEMIOUS LIVING
A CHRISTIAN UNCONCIOUSLY VIBRATES TOWARDS CARNALISM

3. PRAYER ZONE

4. MOURNING
FASTING ZONE

Some folk who have never fasted for longer than a meal or two in their lives, may not care to begin a fast all at once. It is suggested they take four or more days in preparation for the consecration fast TO JESUS in this manner:

15

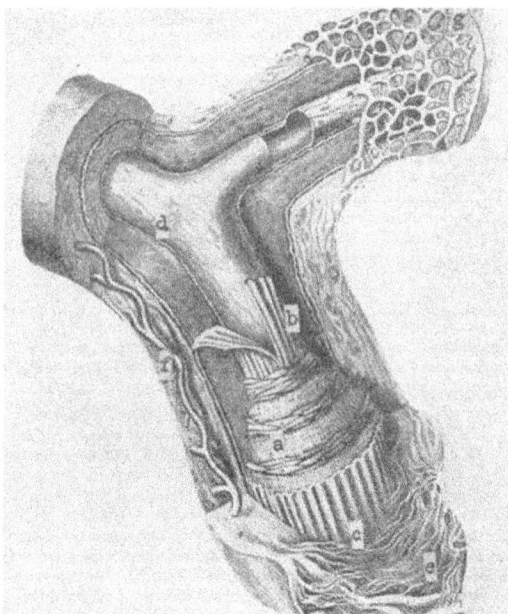

THE CARRIER OF THE LIFE OF THE FLESH

The artery is the blood vessel that carries "THE LIFE OF THE FLESH," our blood. The fate of a human being depends upon the solidity and strength of this life carrier more than on most other things in the human body. The majority of people die as a result of disease of the arterial wall. (a) The muscle fibres are reinforced with alternate layers of connective tissue. (b and c) Elastic fibres unite to form layers which alternate with the muscle fibres. These are elastic fibres which pass between the muscle bundles. They pull the artery together like rubber bands. (d) The inside of the tube also is covered with a layer of flat cells. (e) The outer surface of the artery is covered by loose connective tissue which cushions the impact of the forward, projectile motion of the pulse. (f) These are small accessory blood and lymph-vessels, which supply the cells of the arterial wall with nutrient materials, which pass through this padding. Each artery has its private arteries, and also its intricate system of nerves that regulate the width of the vessel. (g) The capillaries, network of minute vessels fifty times thinner than our hair. The average diameter is 1/3000 of an inch. Blood corpuscles pass through it in single file. Fasting has much to do with the cleansing of these vessels to prevent hardening of the arteries and disease.

FOUR STEPS OF PREPARATION

FOURTH DAY BEFORE THE FAST:—

Leave off all meat and fried foods in diet.

THIRD DAY BEFORE BEGINNING FAST:—

Eat mostly green vegetables, cooked or otherwise.

SECOND DAY BEFORE BEGINNING FAST:—

Eat choice of any live foods. Live foods are any uncooked food, such as vegetables, dried and fresh fruit, nuts, etc. These foods contain the most life giving substances for the body, and contain a plentiful amount of vitamins and minerals. Milk products are also live foods.

FINAL DAY BEFORE BEGINNING FAST:—

A fresh fruit diet. (Tomatoes may be included). Eat all that is desired.

THEN BEGIN FAST THE NEXT DAY.

Approximately one pound of weight is lost daily. Physical work will cause more weight to be lost and, if one is not too weak, it is not detrimental.

AUTOMATIC BLOOD TRANSFUSION:

Out of this pound or so of weight that is lost, the blood is retained within the body along with most of the minerals and necessary vitamins. This is a natural physiological process. After a few days fasting, one may even find it difficult to sleep. The large amount of blood goes into the head, and sometimes fever may result. The brain being bathed with more blood than usual, finds a certain part of the fast difficult, insofar as sleeping is concerned. The organs are consequently bathed in this "life" force. This is one reason one can receive healing through the fast. There is no more natural blood transfusion but that which is obtained through fasting. It requires a long fast for deep seated ailments, glands and other vital organs, to become thoroughly cleansed and purified. This is also true in relation to the removal of the doubts and unbelief.

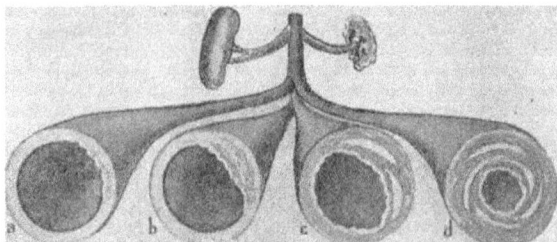

"LIFE" runs through these tubes. Fasting keeps tubes clean. The hardening of these arteries slows down the life flow. When the arteries harden, other organs are affected like the contracted kidney at the right — or the heart.

"For the LIFE OF THE FLESH IS IN THE BLOOD": Lev. 17:11.

If a human being were squeezed out like a lemon, no less than eleven gallons of water would be obtained. The human body is seven-tenths fluid. This is the same proportion of fluids as the earth. The moon, along with the other planets, influence and cause the tidal waves. It is logical to also believe that our fluids, which are even more vital, are influenced by them that are identical, and almost in the same proportion. They are: (1) 80% sodium, (2) 4% calcium, (3) 4% potassium and 2 to 10% (4) magnesium.

This is no ordinary water, but—sea water! It contains the same salts, etc., that sea water contains. Both sea water and the fluid from our bodies contain these FOUR elements.

In diagram (a-d) are shown the changes in the vascular wall which end in calcification: In (a) and (d), we have the first steps in the ulceration and proliferation of connective tissue. When regular systematic fastings are gone into, these conditions cannot come about. At this stage, they can become eradicated in a fast from ten to twenty-one days (fast is to be broken properly). In (c) we notice deposits of calcium; (d) calcification and occlusion of the vessel. Continued regular eating oftentimes consumates the condition in the arteries as shown to right. This could result in scores of sicknesses, such as: cerebral hemorrhage, paralysis, rupture of an artery, rupture of a blood vessel near the heart, heart failure, high blood pressure, etc. Even with the calcium deposits as shown in figure (d), fasting can purify and eradicate these calcium deposits in several short fasts followed by a long fast; the individual will again have the arteries and blood pressure restored to normal. (See "The Fasting Prayer").

We are, of course, presenting the secondary blessings of fasting which concern the tabernacle of the Holy Spirit. The primary blessings are far more essential and important. However, by thoroughly understanding the natural physical part that fasting plays, one will be more bold to go into these fastings more often to please and glorify our Jesus. THIS IS OUR MAIN GOAL.

GIVING THE STOMACH A BATH

If one wishes to hasten into the fast more quickly, a bath can be given the stomach by preparing one quart of very warm water (not too hot); place two level teaspoons full of salt in it and stir. This can be drunk. Usually one has his system flushed out entirely within two hours. This should be taken several hours after the last meal when stomach is empty. One can take this for several days but during the first part of the fast only. The quantity can be increased if necessary. It can also be taken anytime (several hours after eating) when not fasting to keep stomach clean. Some people use this bath daily.

SOLEMN WARNING

Fasting being an anti-pleasure measure, we are not supposed to seek pleasure in it, or to even expect such, other than spiritual pleasure. Because fasting has such a power in connection with the natural things being successfully accomplished when our attention is thus directed to them, we are even forbidden to call this a consecration fast. That is, if one is fasting mainly for greater success in business, or for selfish material welfare, or for healing only, or some other personal object—this is an unacceptable fast to God. "Behold, in the day of your fast ye FIND PLEASURE, and exact all your labours. Behold, ye fast for strife and debate, and to smite with the fist of wickedness: ye shall not fast as ye do this day, to make your voice to be heard on high." Isa. 58:3,4.

A sanctified fast calls for a fast dedicated to Jesus and our whole aim should be unselfish. If our fast has other main objectives aside from Jesus, we are acting presumptuous. We need not worry about our needs and problems. Jesus knows all about them and when the fast has been entered into properly, Jesus will see that we have the desires of our heart.

Fasting is a symbol of mourning, going down into repentance and chastening of the heart. Very little pleasure, if any at all, can be found when seeking the Kingdom of God with this process. When one attempts it, he may be FASTING WRONGLY. According to the above Scripture, it may be possible for one to "FIND PLEASURE" by seeking it when fasting. This is very true during the first part of a fast.

In seeking God, we also cry out, mourn, groan and travail in this type of praying, and the fast will enable us to get away from all natural pleasure. One of the very purposes of the fast is to forsake all pleasures, of which, the eating pleasure is the key stone to all other pleasures, etc.

Fasting is such a powerful spiritual factor in obtaining special favors from our Lord, that we must above all things keep humble when we receive them. Many times the blessings received will surprise our little faith and the devil creeps in with pride, causing us to rise up as if to say, "look what I did," etc.

We do not and cannot claim merit from fasting. Brother Charles E. Robinson has written a tract on fasting. In it he makes this point clear of which we agree:

"This article would be incomplete without a solemn warning. Satan will not fail to tempt the faster to adopt the Pharisaic theory of salvation by merit. Luke 18:11,12. But it was the publican who claimed no merit who was forgiven. Satan moved the Pharisee to think he could bring pressure to bear on God which He, being just, could not resist. He will try to do the same with the faster. God has promised to reward the faithful faster, but this reward is not to be claimed as for merit lest any man should boast. Ephesians 2:8,9. No matter how much or how long we fast we are still unprofitable servants, having merely done our duty. Luke 17:10.

I do know that what I could not get done by praying, with a spell of bilious fever, a 15-day fast—no food but drinking plenty of water—brought me to the place to which Jesus came when He "afterward was an hungered." Matt. 4:2. The 15th day I became hungry, ate, and was well."

Many times Christian people receive some wonderful things from the Lord through sanctified fasting, only to be shorn of all or part of these blessings by permitting pride and boastfulness to creep in. One has also to refrain from too much "appearance" in ourselves after fasting as well as this "appearance" during the fasting period. In everything it should be done for the Glory of God. When this is our entire motive, then our humbleness and victories

20

in fasting can be testified to for the exaltation and praise of Him, who redeemed us from the curse of the law.

THE ACTS OF THE HOLY SPIRIT reveals that prayer, supplications and FASTINGS were largely put into practice. The church was born in the midst of the former rain of the Holy Spirit through men and women who went ALL OUT FOR GOD. This, of course, included the entire, full old time faith which induded the foundation teachings of Jesus Christ of which FASTING WAS ONE of them. The latter rain is under development at the present time, and when enough of Christ's people go all out for Him in Fastings and prayers, contending for ALL of the OLD TIME FAITH, then, surely a mighty revival of power and the operations of the Spirit will become fully manifested.

THE FOUR HIGH POINTS OF SPIRITUAL PROGRESS CAME THRU FASTING AND PRAYER

THE 40 YEAR WILDERNESS

LET UP OF THE OLD TIME FAITH FASTING PRAYERS

1906 / 1946 1947
AZUSA FASTING

1" PENTECOST

MATT 9:15
ACTS 1:14
ACTS 2:35-2:1:
42-47

THE DARK AGES REFORMATION
MARTIN LUTHER AND OTHER REFORMERS FASTED WEEKS AT A TIME

PREPARATION FOR THE LATTER RAIN
JOEL 1 & 2

ALMOST ALIVE

The intestinal canal, containing five million finger-like villi and three thousand cells to each one of these villi, is one of the most wonderful and glorious parts of man that our blessed Creator has created. Our nourishment or nutrition is developed there. It is the fountainhead for the well-being of our body. This digestive tubing has its own nervous system and can continue living approximately four hours after a person passes out of this life and his heart has stopped beating. With these vigorous cells and complicated structure, a piece of the intestinal tract has been kept alive outside of the body, in a warm nutritive solution, for days at a time. When round solid materials were placed into one end of the tubing, it performed its movements in the peristaltic manner, like it does in the body, and completely 'pushed the objects through the tubing. These tests were made several days after a person died. Why not show due respect for this wonderful mechanism of the temple of the Holy Spirit by giving it a vacation more often for the glory of Jesus?

21

The breaking of the fast is a very slow procedure, if one wishes to retain every good thing that was accomplished by it. The prophets and men of old were acquainted with the proper care in the breaking of fasts.

In the study of Elijah's fasts, we notice the angel giving him food in two different installments before he went on his forty-day fast. (I Kings 19:5-8). In the study of Elijah just before the forty-day fast, we see him performing miracles on an empty stomach. Famine was in the land, but Brother Elijah was a very wise prophet who gave "no thought for tomorrow." He took adversity and converted it into glory and honor for the Lord. This very famine that loomed so menacingly to most was immediately changed by Elijah into a consecration fast. When this fast had run its course, the Lord sent ravens to feed him twice daily. Another famine enveloped the stricken land, and we believe he also sanctified this one into a prayerful fast, for it was soon afterward that he performed some notable miracles. At any rate, with the brook, his only source of water dried up, he was led to a very poor widow to break his fast— and, please notice, how careful he was in breaking it. "And when he came to the gate of the city, behold, the widow woman was there gathering of sticks: and he called to her, and said, Fetch me, I pray thee, a little water in a vessel, that I may drink. And as she was going to fetch it, he called to her, and said, Bring me, I pray thee, A MORSEL OF BREAD IN THINE HAND." Please note Elijah's instruction, "A MORSEL of bread." (I Kings 17:10-13). Surely, he was endeavoring to break a fast that he had been on and realized that water was the most important thing, and that a tiny piece of bread carefully eaten would then be the next procedure. Again, we are further shown that, although Elijah had been on a fast in a famished country, he was familiar with the breaking-in procedure because we are told in Verse 13,— "And Elijah said unto her, Fear not; go and do as thou hast said: but make me thereof a LITTLE cake first, and bring it to me, and after make for thee and for thy son." Please notice the miracle after fasting. "The barrel of meal shall not waste, neither shall the cruse of oil fail."

The author feels that Elijah was one of the greatest advocates of fasting who ever lived and equaled only by John the Baptist, his proto type.

In the next chapter of I Kings, we find the God of Elijah answering by fire and the prophets of Baal embarrassingly exposed. Please note that Elijah, evidently, was on a fast here, after this spectacular miracle, because I Kings 18:41,42: "And Elijah said unto Ahab, Get thee up, EAT AND DRINK; for there is a sound of abundance of rain. So Ahab went up to eat and to drink. And Elijah went up to the top of Carmel; and HE CAST HIMSELF DOWN UPON THE EARTH, and put his face between his knees." then we find Elijah out-running Ahab who had been on natural food, while the prophet of God had been on a spiritual feast of faith and power. "And the hand of the Lord was on Elijah; and he girded up his loins, and ran before Ahab." I Kings 18:46.

The food abstentionist, Elijah, had very severe trials along with all of his fasts. Any person will also have severe trials in a consecration fast. This will be a real spiritual fight if you put everything you have into it. Please study the next chapter carefully, and note some of the trying experiences that befell Elijah because he was being used mightily of God in FASTINGS AND PRAYER.

A lesson well learned is the secret behind Elijah's and other great prophets' successes. This is the prophet's-length fast. We, too, can have a prophet's experience by following their example. Why hesitate, why doubt, why dillydally around about it. Let's go into these prophet's-early-church-length of fasting and have their experiences of power and faith. PLEASE REMEMBER THIS, JESUS CHRIST IS NEVER A RESPECTER OF PERSONS. We have just as much right to the miracle working as Elijah had. But we will have to fulfill our part and, sometimes, suffer the miserable conditions that go along with it.

Many times in a Bible Institute, or from among a large group of saints, a person will start fasting for either long or short periods, then break the fast too soon, too rapidly, or mistakenly in some manner, and cause a severe reproach against the power of fasting. Sometimes, the ill effects of their lack of wisdom, is so serious that either they, themselves, will voluntarily go to a hospital or medical man, or some friend will force them to seek the special attention made mandatory by their folly and indiscretion. Because there is little information concerning the subject, all protracted fasting is condemned and barred from the Bible seminary and church. This, of course, frightens people and hinders the progress and advancement of revival power and real Bible experiences.

When we go into a protracted fast without food (water only taken) for a period of days or weeks, the importance of the proper break-fast, after such an interval, is far more important and serious than it would be from supper to the morning meal. The longer the fast the more true this will be. The stomach and intestinal tract go to sleep after a few days of fasting. The digestive and intestinal secretions become retarded and almost at a standstill. To place any solid food into the stomach at this time would be an actual crime against it.

In order to be able to absorb the digested food as well as the large quantities of secreted digestive fluids, the intestinal wall has enlarged its surface by developing not only larger folds, but also minute processes known as VILLI. A high powered lens reveals that the mucous membrane is covered with millions of tiny closely packed, tentacle hair-like structures, called villi. Each villus is from 1/35 to 1/50 of an inch long. These villi become very much smaller in fasting and dormant in action. The longer the fast, the more asleep they seem to become. When in the state of receiving food they appear as in the above diagram. (A) is an empty villus in the act of receiving food, (B) after having received food, and (C) is a villus that has evacuated its contents. (This process is very slow after a long fast). At the upper left may be seen a food particle that has passed into the small intestine in a half-digested condition. When the food comes in contact with the villi beneath it (upper left), the

23

digestive gland knows its requirements and, at once, sends forth a tiny stream (see fountain) of digestive juice over the food to enable it to digest. There is also chemical stimulation to induce the flow of these digestive juices. Wander cells creep out of the lymph node (d) to gnaw at the food and to carry away its insoluble parts. As a result of the digestive action of the glandular secretion, meat is converted into meat water (amino acids), starch into sugar water (grape sugar), and fat into glycerin and SOAP. When fasting a length of time, these glandular secretions rest and go to sleep. When wrong food is placed into them suddenly, and in the wrong manner and quantity, they rebel. They cannot awaken quickly and take up this intricate, delicate task immediately, and abruptly start performing their customary task. Consequently, only a very slow and gradual, gentle stimulation by fruit juices, diluted if the fast is over ten days, and only in small amounts of four to six ounces during the first few meals, is called for. This fruit juice, or clear vegetable water, or clear cereal water, will slowly but gradually reestablish proper digestion and assimilation.

These villi and digestive glands do not dry up and become permanently dormant, but only go to sleep, so to speak, only to be awakened by the very, very light and gentle stimulation of water mingled with a few tiny particles of food, such as would be found in the diluted fruit juices, or clear vegetable waters, on a fast over fifteen days. There would be so small an amount of food particles in this diluted watery food, that they would arouse themselves only very slowly and gradually from their slumber. It might actually take days of this gradually increasing the quantity and strength of food before every one of the cells of the five million villi that are in the intestinal canal (wall) has become fully awakened. Each villi, of the five million, has three thousand cells that have to become fully reawakened before the stomach can be considered fully readjusted to complete normalcy. Consequently, a great deal of time is required and much patience, before the fasting candidate can get his teeth into the full-eating regime again. It usually requires as long to break in a fast as the length that one fasted, but it only takes about six days of the fruit juices and fruit when breaking a fast from twenty-one to forty days. The rest of the days one should eat lightly of easily digested foods, fruits, vegetables or milk, in moderate quantities, properly spaced—and no between meal eating.

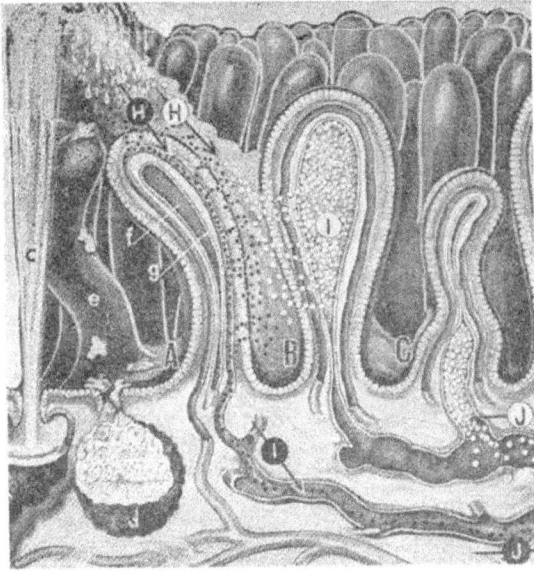

The Intestinal Digestive Apparatus

Within the villus there are two sets of pipes, the blood—and the lymph— vessels. The blood-vessels are located externally and absorb both amino acids and sugar. These two classes of substances pass by way of the path 1, 2, 3 into the blood-stream. The lymph-vessels end as narrow bags (f). These bags suck themselves full of glycerin and soap (H), from which they form human fat, so that the nutritive fluid is transformed into a kind of milk. 'When the villus has become filled with milk (I), it contracts and pushes the milk into the lymph-vessels (J). Villi can be seen pumping milk down into lymph-vessels.

WE DO NOT LIVE ON WHAT WE EAT

Man does not live on what he eats, but rather on what he digests. The body is not nourished by what is put into the food cavity, but by what passes through and around the FIVE MILLION VILLI.

Everyone eats, and everyone thinks he knows why he eats. Medical science does not know why, and does not yet know what a cell is, neither does it know in what manner this cell motor transforms the food substance which it receives into energy. Therefore, it is also unable to say why man eats, and why the cell requires just these and no other food substances in order to function properly physically. The fact remains that no doctor or scientist has ever offered a satisfactory answer, Jesus Christ showed to us the most perfect way. He revealed to us that not only must man give attention to his physical requirements, but he also had a far more important part of himself that needed and also required special attention. This was his spiritual nature. He gave us a lesson in this regard in Matthew 4:4: "Man shall not live by bread alone, but by every word that proceedeth out of the mouth of God." He was speaking of food abstention because He had just completed a prophet's-length fast. (Compare Deut. 8:3).

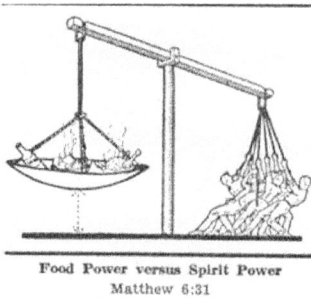

Food Power versus Spirit Power
Matthew 6:31

Some religious groups are typical of a body of toilers who get nothing accomplished. While they are doing a lot of hard work they labor in vain. On the left of the illustration, we have represented our continued three meal a day stuffing habit. On the right, is depicted lukewarm Christians, attached, bound, and so occupied with these "weights" as if their very lives depended upon these instead of Christ. A close observation reveals that their whole body, soul and mind is taken up entirely with the procedure. They would not have strength, or time, for other spiritual things. The buying, preparation, cooking, serving and eating of food keeps many a person from HAVING TIME TO PRAY LET ALONE FAST. Should I say, have time to fast? Actually, this would be a laughable excuse because unless one has a large family, to cook and care for, one would have a lot more time to fast. If these laborers would only let loose of the strings and encumbrances they are attached to, they would immediately and automatically be on a fast. Why strain, work and pant about a lot of things that, after all, are not really necessary all of the time? Please see Matthew 6:25; Luke 10:40-42; Psalm 78.

PASTOR ON TWENTIETH DAY OF FAST

Dear Brother Hall:

I am pleased that Jesus has enabled me to be on my twentieth day of fasting. I know it is a deeper experience for all of us who will pay the price. It is the real secret of revival success.

May Jesus bless you, Pastor Harold O'Brien

26

Bowmanvill, Ontario, Canada.

We are giving some testimonies from people who have become moderate in their every day living by going into consecrated fastings to please Jesus:

34 Day Fast Unto God May Have Saved

Me From Injury in Car Accident

Dear Rev. Hall:

Greetings in Jesus Precious Name:

I have come off my thirty four day complete fast without food. The first week after the fast another car crashed right into my car. I was shook up some but I was not hurt. I have been acquainted with your teachings on the Holy Ghost and Fire Protection power. Although I did not see the Glory Cloud, I did see the tiny flames and I could feel them cover my body with protection power when the accident occurred. Please let me know in July when You have the Holy Ghost and Fire Seminar. I want to plan on attending.

Thank the Lord for what Fasting and Prayer along with the Holy Ghost and Fire will do. I just seem to feel the tingling sensation more around me when I fast.

I hope to hear from you soon.

Evangelist Darthenia Green, Pittsburgh, Pa.

Dear Brother Hall:

Greetings to you in Jesus dear name.

I am happy that the Lord has given to you such a wonderful fasting and Holy Ghost Fire Healing ministry.

When your last letter came, I had a Pneumonia Temperature of more than one hundred three degrees. I placed your letter upon my head and shouted "Hallelujah", immediately the fever broke. The Touch of the Lord came upon me. Sorry I am so short of money to send to you this time. Pray that God loosens funds for me.

In Jesus.

Irene Tyler, Freedom, California

27

AFTER FASTING TWENTY-ONE DAYS

BROTHER CAN IMPART HOLY GHOST FIRE BAPTISM

AND OPERATES GIFT OF FAITH

Dear Brother and Sister Hall:

I want to thank the Lord for sending you both to Chicago. The Lord has greatly blessed me since I have come into the Bodyfelt Salvation Fasting Ministry. My wife sees so much more to this ministry. She sees that I have more energy and have more joy and many other wonderful changes the Lord has brought upon me. Now my wife is beginning to turn to the Lord, praise Jesus.

The Lord has blessed me to enter into two twenty-one day fasts. These fasts, just bring more of the Holy Ghost Clothing of Power upon my body.

BARBER WORKS AND FASTS TWENTY-EIGHT DAYS

RECOUNTS HEALINGS

Thank Jesus forever. He is mine and I feel Him ever so near me. It seems like everything unlike Him is entirely conquered, and I have entirely sold out to Him by giving away completely to His Holy Spirit.

Although I only fasted twenty-eight days, the experience is the best I have ever had in Him. I worked every day at the barber chair, preached three times a week, and prayed at meal time in place of eating. Then, at night, I really prayed and also in the prayer meetings.

This is seventeen days after the "break-fast" period and I followed directions very carefully in this matter of adjusting the stomach to food again. This evening there was a birthday dinner for me, but I ate sparingly and stopped eating when I should. Fasting will help us to put the proper value on food.

JOURNAL-GAZETTE

FORT WAYNE, INDIANA, THURSDAY MORNING, OCTOBER 30, 1947   PRICE FIVE

Consecrated Fasting Bringing
About Physical Blessing
Converts Toxemia and
Most Sicknesses into Food
Fuel for Its Own Destruction

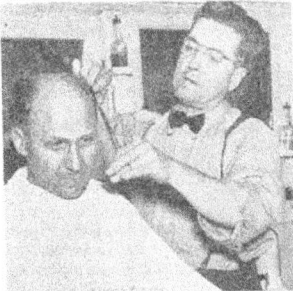

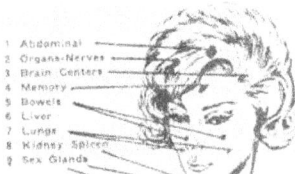

Customer E. M. Burts and Barber Glenn Espich, the 28-day dieter

LOST 33 POUNDS

Barber Without Food 28 Days In Religious Fast

By RAY SCHERER

There's one man in our town who has really gone all out of President Truman's food saving program. Two hundred per cent in fact.

Glenn T. Espich of 476 Elizabeth Street is the man. Last night he gorged himself on three spoonfuls of orange juice—his first food in 28 days.

Mr. Espich is an ordained clergyman of the Fundamental Christian Church. He preaches here and tends a neighborhood barber shop at 250 East State Boulevard, just west of Barter's Garage.

On the first of October he scaled 208 pounds. Last night, while bubbling up his bottle, Mr. Espich weighed in at 175. That's down 33 pounds in 28 days of occasional sips of water.

The 55-year-old preacher-barber proclaimed it a religious fast. "I was scared to do it and I really didn't know how far I'd get," he says.

Based on the Bible (fasted 31 days and Elijah went for 40.

Mr. Espich says he was asked the Almighty to "send us a revival." He declares he wanted the young people to go to church and sing this combination.

Gandhi-like stunt which ended last night. "I went on working in the shop every day though. Finally I got so weak I had to push myself to work. Last Sunday was the day I got the hungriest. I was only three days away from my goal so I didn't weaken," he explains.

Fast Disciple

Mr. Espich is a disciple of San Diego's Franklin Hall, the nation's foremost fast advocate. "He got our women to go 62 days," Dr. worldwide acclaim world he reports.

"I'll be on oranges juice for about five days, then some vegetables then I'm on any meal for another 28 day.

The customers have told him that the new 175 pounds looks good on the 5 foot 7 Espich frame. Espich agrees he feels good but weak. Clothes don't fit anymore but he has barbed his trousers up in the back with safety pins.

(Tried Gold, Rev. 3:18)

1 Abdominal
2 Organs-Nerves
3 Brain Centers
4 Memory
5 Bowels
6 Liver
7 Lungs
8 Kidney Spleen
9 Sex Glands

By reflex action — sicknesses
are also reflected in feet.

Acts
2:19

SPIRIT
No More Sin
SOUL
No More Sickness
BODY

Here are the facts as I remember them: The first four days were difficult, then hunger left me. Some people were praying for me who knew I was fasting, and this strengthened me immensely. On the tenth day I had lost fifteen pounds. I was not worried any time during the

29

fast. Some Christians encouraged me to go on. I was able to pray for a crippled child who lives near me and Jesus touched her little body on the twenty-first day of the fast. The child now walks every where. The father and mother are saying Jesus did it. A bed-fast brother was prayed for, and he immediately got up healed. November ninth, I was taken to a hospital to pray for a man who had typhoid fever and the Lord came on the scene like a bolt of lightning and healed him.

My eyesight is fifty percent better, arthritis has left my body and there are no more aches in my arms.

Some pie-chicken loving preachers here in "Wayne" said I was after glamour and publicity. I could not help it if folk knew I was fasting, besides, I was only fasting to Jesus. Anyway, people made fun of David when he fasted and he did not care—neither do I. (Psalm 109:24,25). 1 told them, people also knew that Jesus and Johns' disciples also fasted.

After Jesus fasted, Satan came on the scene and gave Him a battle. I also had opposition and spiritual warfare but Jesus brought me through. Fasting is POWER and it has enabled me to claim victory and believe through on what I have been praying about.

I also found out that good drinking water has a lot to do with fasting and it is better to drink it warm than too cold after we get on into the fast. Chlorine water is obnoxious and very disagreeable to take.

Tepid enemas were taken every three days and this proved helpful in many ways. To keep my breath pure and cleansed, while working with my barber customers, I touched my tongue to some tiny menthol crystals. I did not use gum or sen sen.

The last is best. My daughter gave birth to a beautiful baby girl (six pounds, twelve ounces) in three and one-half hours. I travailed for her in prayer while fasting for thirty minutes. Praise the Lord it was worth any sacrifice I tried to make. Jesus does reward us and oftentimes, the fasting rewards are full of pleasant surprises.

Yours in the Lord, Brother Glenn Espich

Fort Wayne, Indiana.

REVIVALS THROUGH FASTING AND PRAYER

Dear Brother Hall:

Many people started fasting for a city-wide revival and some great meetings came into our city. We saw wonderful results that fasting and prayer accomplished. I believe nearly three hundred people became converted. I am glad I received light on this wonderful Bible fasting truth. I went into more and longer fasts and we have seen God do some wonderful healings.

I sent the fasting book, "Atomic Power With God" to my son in Tulsa, Olda., who is in Bible college, and he fasted six days. My sister who is also there, fasted for nine days, and a mighty revival has broken out in that area. Thank Jesus for revivals coming this way in answer to fasting and prayer.

Sister E. N. Hawk, Hamilton, Ohio.

THE ULTIMATE GOAL AND ACCOMPLISHMENT OF THE CROSS HAS NEVER BEEN REACHED BECAUSE. . . ONLY THE SHAME OF THE CROSS HAS EVER DARED TO BE PREACHED

Glory of the Cross

THE THREE MEN, RECORDED, TO HAVE FASTED 40 DAYS DEMONSTRATED THE GLORY OF THE CROSS! Moses received Bodyfelt Salvation SUBSTANCE GLORY OF THE LORD UPON HIS PERSON. Elijah received the Glory of the Cross Substance so mightily upon himself that he was translated without seeing death. Jesus Christ, who found it necessary to empty Himself first of His Shekinah Glory, paying the COST-PRICE SHAME OF THE CROSS, then afterwards arose from the dead; BUT HIS RESURRECTION WAS NOT ENOUGH, it was likewise necessary for Him to get back up into His glory and be thereby reestablished in it that we too may possess the protective glory of the cross substance which is the kingdom of Heaven Glory.

PROPER CONSECRATED

FASTING enables the Lord's people to properly DISCERN THE LORD'S BODY (1 Cor. 11:29,30) The Lord's glory body from attaining the glory of the cross from His ascension back up in glory. His expedient return to glory that He could bring it back to us through the Holy Spirit full baptism.

Only one part of our salvation has seemingly been taught. The sin problem, eliminated by Jesus' shed blood, The "SHORTNESS OF GLORY" portion (See Romans

31

3:23) "For all have sinned, (this portion taught over and over) and come short of the glory of God;" The latter portion is the most important for full redemption attainment, yet it has deplorably been left out.

Attention was called to the reader above. At least three persons who fasted much did enter into a portion if not all of the "shortness of glory" covering Comforter Baptism of Holy Ghost Fire! The restoration of lost Garments of Adam and Eve. "The Garments of Salvation" (Is. 61:10) The "glory that is seen upon one" (Is. 60:1-5, 21, 22) also the protective ingredients (illustrated above) outlined in Isaiah 4:5: (1) CLOUD, (2) SMOKE, (3) FIRE, (4) and LIGHT.

FASTING RESULTS:

THIS IS THE MOST IMPORTANT TEACHING IN THIS VOLUME

Fasting properly unto our Lord brings forth the glory of the cross, enabling God's people to come into full realization that we may also obtain a fundamental Bodyfelt as well as the fundamental Heartfelt salvation experience. THE PROMISE OF THE FATHER TO COME UPON US. (Lk. 24:49, Acts 1:4,8; 2:3, 17, 19, Rev. 3:17, 18 etc.) Salvation in our heart is not enough. Salvation upon us heals, protects from all harm and is accident sickness prevention!

This is Jesus' teaching in the Sermon on the Mount. The Lord's prayer is contained in this same chapter and Christians are conscious of praying, but fail to give heed to His teachings concerning fasting and proper eating. In this chapter, there are more verses of scripture dealing with fasting and eating than there are prayer and also of alms (giving). Why not put all of Jesus' teachings into practice?

33

FASTING BRINGS REVIVAL WITHOUT AN EVANGELIST

Dear Doctor Hall:

am so very thankful for the light on fasting and prayer. I never before realized the great possibilities contained in this great truth. After just ending a ten-day fast and seeing marvelous accomplishments, I have been encouraging different ones in the church to try fasting and prayer as the answer to some very difficult problems. I am especially encouraged with the wonderful victory I have had in my personal life through the FASTING PRAYER.

Many of our people are becoming interested and are now fasting.

We had an EVANGELIST WITHOUT MUCH OF A REVIVAL BEFORE OUR FASTING, BUT NOW WE ARE HAVING A REVIVAL WITHOUT AN EVANGELIST. . Thank Jesus that fasting will draw us close to His bosom.

Your sister in Jesus,

Lucile Farmer, Superior, Wyoming.

SUFFERED TEN MONTHS—HEALED AFTER SERIES OF SHORT FASTS

Dear Brother Hall:

Fasitng and prayer is God's way for His people, and it is one hundred percent Biblical. Two doctors told me they could do nothing for me but offered pills and medicine. I had heart specialists tell me there was but little hope. After fasting five to seven days, five times within seventy-five days, Jesus completely delivered me of my affliction. I had gone down to death's door and prayed earnestly, and Jesus gave me the Holy Spirit. Still, I was not healed until I took the series of fasts.

I assure you there is nothing to fear, and I believe it is God's way for an old fashioned white HOT Holy Ghost Revival.

I regret to say I have seen too many preachers that would eat like hogs, and these gluttons would fight and oppose fasting. God help such ignorant people who are supposed to be helping others, but, instead, are defeating their own purpose. The world is filled with these overstuffed backsliding folk.

Brother Jacobson

Burt, Iowa.

SPIRITUAL AND PHYSICAL WEIGHTS OF UNCLEANLINESS

Many of us are not aware of the tremendous weights and of the great hindrances caused by being on a continued feeding habit

These unnecessary weights make us the enemies of the cross.

"I told you often and now tell you even weeping, that they are the enemies of the cross of Christ: whose end is destruction, whose God is their belly, who mind earthly things" II Cor. 4:17.

Are you too carrying unnecessary burdens, weights and obstacles because of food diseases?

As the illustration shows, Field Marshall Gallas actually carried his excess weight, his fat abdomen in a wheel barrow. Many Christians, unknowingly, are carrying their weight hindrances unnecessarily around. Not unnecessarily the weights of excess fat abdomen in a wheelbarrow, that prevent them from running in the race of God! These natural and evil unbelief weights hinder us from carrying the proper "WEIGHTS OF GLORY" II Cor. 4:17.

PLEASURE EMOTIONS

CAPACITY FOR THE ENJOYMENT OF PLEASURE

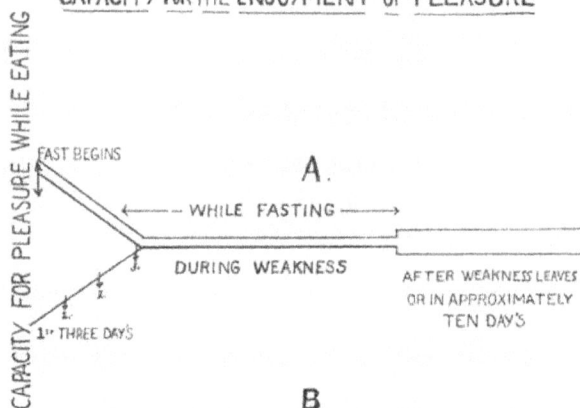

CAPACITY FOR PLEASURE WHILE EATING

FAST BEGINS

A.

← — WHILE FASTING ——→

DURING WEAKNESS

AFTER WEAKNESS LEAVES
OR IN APPROXIMATELY
TEN DAYS

1ˢᵗ THREE DAYS

B.

CAPACITY FOR THE SPIRITUAL

→ INNER REVIVAL

DURING AND AFTER FASTING

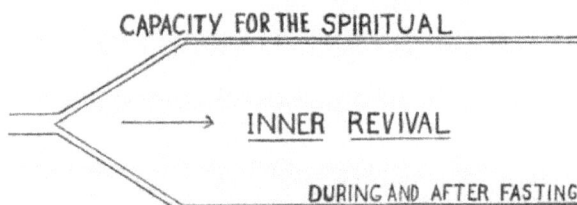

WHEN GOING ON A HUNGER STRIKE FOR THE GLORY OF JESUS, WE ALSO STRIKE OUT SATANIC INFLUENCES AND WORLDLY PLEASURE. OUR CAPACITY FOR THE SPIRITUAL, THEN, BECOMES AS GREAT AS IT HAD BEEN FOR THE NATURAL. (A) SHOWS PLEASURE AND THE LUSTS OF THE FLESH AT A STANDSTILL. (B) DEPICTS THE FLESH ARRESTED. IT CANNOT GO ON A RAID WHILE FASTING. AN INNER REVIVAL IS THE RESULT. THE FLESH AND THE SPIRIT ARE AT ENMITY WITH EACH OTHER.

THE WORLD NUMBER 4 PLAYS AN IMPORTANT PART,
IN THE STUDY OF THE FAST. FOUR IS THE NUMBER OF
HUMANITY. IN THE PHYSIOLOGICAL STUDY OF MAN, WE
FIND FOUR MANIFESTING ITSELF IN MANY WAYS. FOUR
IS VERY MUCH RELATED TO THE SUBJECT OF FASTING AS
THE READER SHALL PRESENTLY SEE. WE ARE ALSO
INCLUDING OTHER INTERESTING FOURS FOR STUDY.

THE 4 ESSENTIALS IN ORDER OF THEIR IMPORTANCE	THE 4 APPETITES EVERY NORMAL PERSON HAS THESE	THE 4 APPETITES BEFORE FASTING	THE 4 APPETITES AFTER FASTING
1. AIR	1. HUNGER	1. HUNGER	1. HUNGER
2. SLEEP	2. SEX	2. SEX	2. SEX
3. WATER	3. GREED	3. GREED COVETOUSNESS	3. GREED
4. FOOD	4. SPIRITUAL	4 SPIRITUAL	4. SPIRITUAL

SINCE MORE THAN NINETY-FIVE PERCENT OF OUR POPULATION
ARE AUTO-INTOXICATED WITH FOOD, HOW CAN WE OVER-STRESS
THE SUBJECT OF FASTING. ALMOST WITHOUT EXCEPTION, JESUS
CONDEMNED OVER EATING AND SURFEITING, ALONG WITH DRINK-
ING, EVEN PLACING IT AHEAD OF DRINKING. MOST DRUNKARDS
BECOME FOOD DRUNKARDS FIRST. ALCOHOLISM CAN NOT SUR-
VIVE A SEIGE OF FASTING. FOOD DRUNKARDS BECOME DISEASED.

THE FOUR TASTES

The food abstentionist denies the pleasures of taste when fasting. The tongue is the first part of the stomach. There are four taste zones or pits in the tongue. These are located at different points on the tongue as shown on the diagram. These taste zones are: (1) sweet, (2) salt, (3) sour, (4) bitter. The zones are not sharply separated, but overlap. In the center of the tongue is a zone that has no taste pit bud, and consequently tastes nothing: this is the silent zone. Try tasting something sweet on the back of the tongue or salt on the tip of the tongue and find how devoid of the real taste they are! Almost all our foods are composed of various substances, and consequently, stimulate not one but several, often even all four taste mechanisms, thus producing the mixed sensations of taste. A lemon has a bitter as well as a sour taste; an apple is sour and sweet at the same time. On the front part of the tongue alum produces a sour taste, while on the back it creates a sweetish taste. There is no such thing as a pure taste. The tongue perceives not only a sweet or a saline sensation, but also the weight, fluidity, roughness or smoothness, mildness or sharpness, temperature, viscidity, and volatility of food.

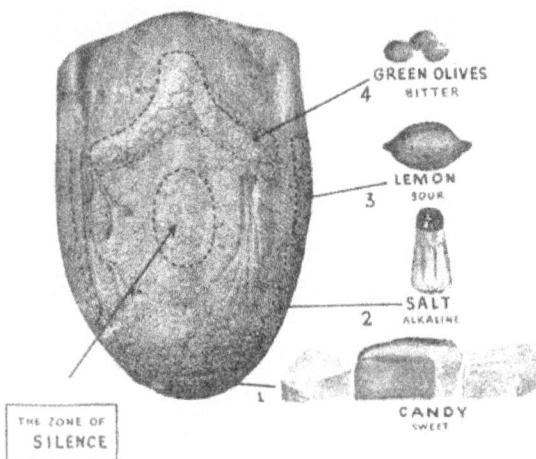

When these taste buds are given a vacation, a new spiritual stronger taste, is acquired for the deeper things of Jesus. This seems to be a resurrection of the deliciousness of the Spirit.

Taste means enjoyment. As we have stated, fasting is an anti-pleasure process. Likewise, we sacrifice the enjoyment of tasting the many dishes that we would enjoy while eating naturally.

"0 taste and see that the Lord is good." Psalm 34:8.

Fasting gives us a better opportunity to "FEAST" on the goodness of the Lord.

When we once taste the good works and Words of God, we enjoy having regular and frequent tastes of His righteousness. "If so be ye have tasted that the Lord is gracious." I Peter 2:3.

Some kinds of food are not so pleasant to taste. Vinegar and salt are very unpleasant to taste by themselves. Likewise, some parts of the Gospel are disagreeable to taste. The message of fasting is one of the most difficult to taste and receive. Jesus partook of this process for forty long days. He went into every kind of misery that can be encountered by all fasting people. He tasted every phase of it. He not only entered into and tasted of fasting, but He also went further and "TASTED DEATH FOR EVERY MAN." Hebrews 2:3. In this, He tasted every awful disagreeable thing imaginable.

Let us remember that we can more effectively taste of the spiritual when we go into food abstention for a time.

DECEPTIVE TASTES

Many times children do not eat certain foods because they imagine they are not good. Sometimes adults are also misled this way, only to find out after tasting and eating a dish, they were mistaken. Some adults have lived longer than fifty years without trying a certain dish, only to find after giving it a thorough try that it was very delicious. How disappointed they were when finding they had lost out, usually through delusion, the enjoyment of a lovely dish for so long a period!

This also applies spiritually with the word of God. There could be many vital subjects in the Word of God that we may not have tasted. Fasting may he one of them, not necessarily a fast of only two or three days. but the prophet's-early church-length fasts. This may also include the Jesus-length fast. Any average person can go into these various lengths of Lists.

Why not taste and see?

At one time the author handled many kinds of flavoring extracts. Flavor will fool one by taste. A very strong vanilla flavoring, will taste nasty right out of the bottle. A weak low priced flavor will taste better because it is weaker and usually sweetened. The sweetened taste operates upon more of the taste faculty on the tongue, whereby the stronger vanilla has only a strong bitter taste. When the weaker and cheaper vanilla was used in cooking, the housewife was often fooled. The cake or pastry was not well flavored. To overcome the competition of the cheaper grades of flavoring sold by competitors, I would add four drops of my stronger flavoring to a glass of milk slightly sweetened with sugar. After tasting, any housewife would be convinced of both the quality and strength of my product, because she would know how it would taste if used in her own cooking at home.

If fasting and prayer is in the Bible, why not taste it and put it into actual practice in our own lives and be convinced through experience and by the Spirit.

THE 4 DIMENSIONS THESE MAY HAVE SOME RELATIONSHIP TO THE OTHER FOURS	THE 4 DIVISIONS OF THE ALIMENTARY CANAL	THE 4 GOSPEL DIVISIONS	THE 4 TASTES
1. WIDTH	1. MOUTH	1. SALVATION	1. SWEET
2. LENGTH	2. STOMACH	2. BAPTISM	2. SALT
3. HEIGHT	3. SMALL INTESTINE	3. DIVINE HEALING	3. SOUR
4 THE 4TH DIMENSION	4. LARGE INTESTINE	4. COMING KING	4. BITTER

THE SPIRITUAL BALANCE SHEET

Brillat-Savarin begins his famous "PHYSIOLOGY OF TASTE" with the statement: "An animal feeds; man eats; a civilized person dines." This sounds like Luke 21:34 and Matt.

24:38, where the world will be "eating" and "drinking" when the Son of Man comes. If the above was reversed and man would feed himself, instead of living to dine, he could be more glorifying to God Almighty. There is no wrong when eating to live, but living to eat, and without fasting, too, can be very grieving to God's Spirit. The animals feed and they live eight times their growth period because they are fed that which is necessary. Man, on the other hand, is the shortest lived of all creatures, we seldom live more than three limes our growth period.

SISTER OF SIXTY-EIGHT FASTS FORTY DAYS

Dear Sir:

I am sixty-eight years of age and have broken a forty-day consecration fast. I am so happy that Jesus completely healed me of many things. I can praise Him for healing me of high blood pressure, cardiac asthma, and female trouble so serious I could not have been relieved except through a surgical operation.

Thank the Lord for giving you the revelation to put out such a "masterpiece" on the subject. Many would be willing to fast, but do not know how to do so intelligently. All glory be to the Father, Son and Holy Ghost.

Mrs. Minnie Graham

Box 72, Blackburn, Oklahoma.

41

THE 4 HUNGERS (FASTING MASTERS THESE)	THE 4 PARTS OF FASTING	THE 4 NATURAL THINGS TO DO	THE 4 METHODS OF ELIMINATION
1. TRUE HUNGER NATURAL	1. FIRST 3 DAYS HUNGER	1. KEEP CLEAN WASH FACE DRINK WATER ENAMAS	1. LUNGS NOSTRILS
2. HABIT HUNGER LUST HUNGER WHICH IS SIN	2. NEXT 10 DAYS WEAKNESS	2. KEEP IN THE RIGHT FRAME OF MIND	2. SKIN
3. HUNGER OF THE OLD MAN CARNALITY	3. ROUTINE EXPERIENCE	3. GET PLENTY OF SLEEP	3. BOWELS
4. HUNGER FOR PLEASURE	4. HUNGER RETURNS FAST ENDS	4. BREAK THE FAST PROPERLY	4. KIDNEYS

CANADIAN HEALED OF LARGE GROWTH

AFTER FASTING TWENTY-THREE DAYS

We have been greatly helped and blessed by your books on fasting and prayer. We have given away many copies and are now ordering another quantity. Many folk are waiting and hungry for this message up here in Canada.

Many have been blessed through protracted Bible fasting. We, also, have seen what the power of fasting will do in our lives. I had a large tumor or growth in my breast. Several in our family set our hearts to God in fastings. My son fasted for twenty-one days, my husband fasted for twenty-six days and I fasted for twenty-three days for the glory of Jesus. I was gloriously and miraculously healed. In many other ways we were so blessed spiritually, revived and filled anew in a greater way with the Holy Spirit than ever before.

In His service,

Grace M. Peifrey

THE 4	THE 4	THE 4	THE 4
TRIPLET DIVISIONS OF MAN	PIVOTS IN THE ZODIAC	ELEMENTS	KINGDOMS
1. HEAD THROAT LUNGS	1. ARIES	1. FIRE	1. MINERAL
2. STOMACH HEART ABDOMEN	2. CANCER	2. WATER	2. VEGETABLE
3. KIDNEYS GENERATIVE LIVER	3. LIBRA	3. AIR	3 ANIMAL
4. KNEES ANKLES FEET	4. CAPRICORN	4. EARTH	4. SPIRITUAL

HEALED OF GALL BLADDER TROUBLE

AFTER SHORT FAST OF SEVEN DAYS

Jesus healed me just for fasting and praying seven days. I had been suffering for a long time with gall bladder and liver trouble. Jesus delivered me, and I believe He will heal any sick person if he or she will give up everything. including food, and trust Him.

Elder R. A. Bradshaw

Granite City, Ill.

THE 4 NECESSITIES PEOPLE MUST HAVE TO GET WELL	THE 4 BIG RESULTS OF CONSECRATED FASTING	THE 4 IMPORTANT THINGS AFTER FASTING	THE 4 GREAT OBSTACLES REMOVED
1. CONSERVE ENERGY	1. CLEANSED	1. EAT ONLY WHAT IS NECESSARY AFTER THE FAST IS BROKEN RIGHT	1. UNBELIEF
2. PURE BLOOD	2. PHYSICAL REJUVENATION OF THE BODY	2. KEEP BELIEVING WITH PATIENCE	2. LUST UNCLEANNESS
3. PERFECT CIRCULATION OF BLOOD	3. REVELATION	3. ONE NOW HAS A BETTER INSIGHT TO WORD OF GOD READ IT MUCH	3. PRIDE
4. HOPE – FAITH FASTING WILL BRING ALL THESE ABOUT	4. ANSWERED PRAYER MORE POWER WITH GOD	4. BE A MISSIONARY ENLIGHTEN OTHERS TO THIS GREAT TRUTH	4. SPIRITUAL DISTORTION DIVISIONS IN THE BODY OF CHRIST

SHORT FAST OF SIX DAYS DOES WONDERS FOR BODY

Pear Brother Hall:

Not so very long ago a tract fell into my hands on fasting that I liked very much.

I am in the evangelistic field constantly and pray for the sick. If one is to have a great deal of success in praying for the sick, I believe they must fast a lot. At least, I find it so in my ministry.

Fasting is a method to insure revival success and, at present. I am in one here. At first, the people did not want to accept fasting as it is taught in the Bible, but the Holy Ghost caine on the scene and they are accepting it now. After a recent six-day fast I entered into, I find it certainly has done wonders for my body.

Remember, I am the evangelist that conducted a revival for your brother, Virgil Hall, a few years ago. Please give Brother and Sister Virgil Hall my regards.

Your sister in the bonds of Calvary,

Evangelist Thelma Nickel

Bixby, Oklahoma.

OTHER THINGS LOST

PUTTING THE FAST IN A TEST TUBE

S P I R I T U A L		AFTER A PARTIAL OR SHORT FAST	AFTER A PROPHET'S LENGTH FAST
UNBELIEF CARNALITY	FOOD FILTH of DISEASES	★ S P I R I T U A L ★	★ S P I R I T U A L ★
MATT. 17:21 SPIRITUAL UNCLEANLINESS	LUKE 21:34 PHYSICAL UNCLEANLINESS	THAT WHICH IS LOST OR GAINED POWER & MORE POWER	

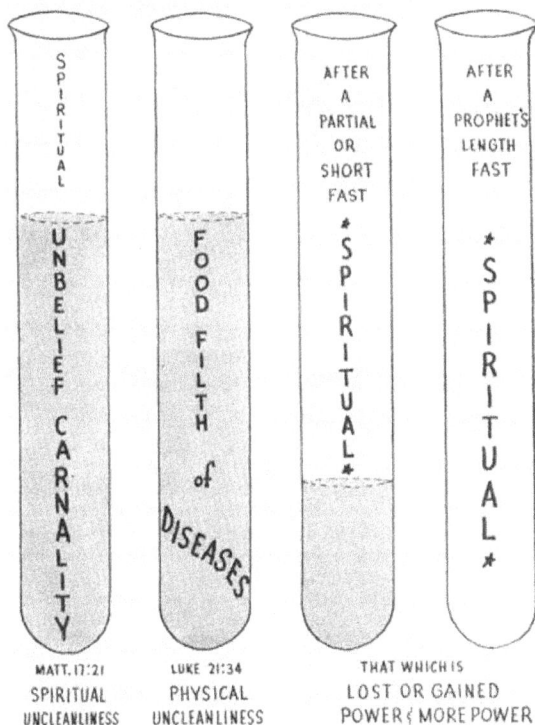

FOOLISH SURFEITERS

Luke 21:34

45

People are eternally looking for some mystifying intelligence that will take care of their ailments and ALLOW THEM TO CONTINUE THEIR SINS AND BAD HABITS. Take, for instance, cathartics, laxatives, and so-called physics. They do not have power to move the bowels. The irritating drugs they contain force the bowels to eliminate the source of irritation and, at the same time, the waste. How much better to conserve energy through FASTING and proper eating so that your body may function under its own power, and eliminate waste naturally without the necessity of harmful prodding. When drugs are taken, the body always has to recover twice instead of only once. It has to overcome the trouble for which the medicine was given, and, later on, it has to recover from the poisonous effects of the drug taken. The drug does not work on the body; rather, the body MUST TAKE CARE OF THE DRUG.

The divine healing that Jesus gives in answer to fasting and prayer is willingly bestowed upon all His children when UNBELIEF IS CAST OUT. If there have been eating habits contrary to the welfare of the body, and the glory of Jesus, the consecrated fast will also chasten the person and undo the wrongs of intemperance while enroute to building up the faith that is necessary to ELIMINATE UNBELIEF. The great WORK OF FASTING always operates in a two-fold manner, physical and spiritual. There is no use in trying to make it work any other way.

Some people believe that certain drugs will cure their colds. Instead of a cure here is what actually happens: When a body is going through a period of ELIMINATION, such as when a cold is present, and is forced to take care of some other unnatural condition, such as drugs and additional amounts of food, the cold will, for the time, be suppressed, or put to one side, so that the body can take care of the new condition that has been forced upon it. However, the cold has not been cured. It is now in a chronic stage, lying latent, affecting the weakest organs of the body. That is the procedure that most chronic invalids have passed through. The suppression of the cold, which was not cured, later on develops into some condition such as bronchitis. Again the attempt is made to cure the ailment in the same erroneous way. The bronchitis is suppressed for a time, only to develop into hay fever or pneumonia later. This, in time, further weakens the affected organs. The final effort of the body to eliminate the poisons and FILTH FROM OVER EATING is through a condition which may be called asthma, and by this time other ailments may have also developed. MOST CHRONIC CONDITIONS ARE THE DEVELOPMENT OF AILMENTS WHICH HAVE BEEN SUPPRESSED IN THE PAST.

When one enters a protracted season of FASTING, these suppressed ills come out into the open again. The physical weaknesses felt in the fast are usually nothing more than many hidden and suppressed afflictions being expelled in the form of eliminations. The weaknesses are the suppressions carried into the blood stream, and the blood is carrying these very poisons out into the proper channels of elimination. These hidden sicknesses must come OUT into the open to become eradicated. When they come to a head in fasting it is similar to a boil coming to a head and the subsequent removal of the core.

It is unpleasant, but how wonderful the person feels after the ordeal! Fasting works along the same line. It is a miserable, painful, trying experience while in the process, but it is so wonderful, both spiritually and physically afterward.

The headache that is often felt during fasting is also an indication the fast:

is needed from the physical standpoint. Coffee drinkers suffer more severe headaches than those who do not have the habit. The caffeine from the coffee comes OUT OF SUPPRESSION and into the bloodstream. The blood circulates the poisons within the head and pain is the natural result. In a few days, the fast will have removed the cause and the headache disappears. Later on as the FAST PROCEEDS to clean up the temple of the Holy Spirit, even the weaknesses, in many instances, disappear, and to one's astonishment the person usually feels better and stronger than he did while indulging in the three or four meal a day stuffing habit, believe it or not.

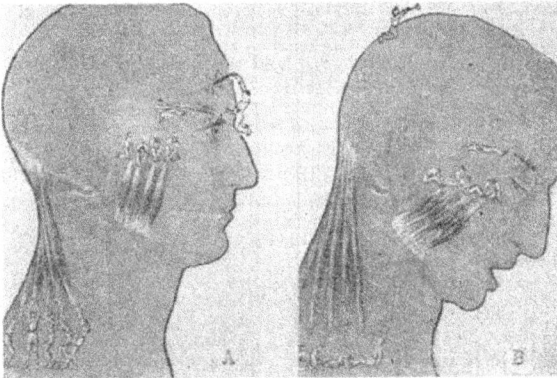

DEMONS CAN BE CAST OUT BY FASTING PRAYER

Matthew 17:21. "This kind goeth not out but by prayer and fasting." The lesson in this chapter was mainly dealing with faith and "Because of your unbelief." The secondary part of the story had to do with demons. However, Jesus teaches IIIs followers that not only the casting out of demons but, "NOTHING SHALL BE IMPOSSIBLE UNTO YOU." This includes power for all things if we follow His formula. The above illustration shows the author's conception of the average person who is afflicted—these afflictions being demon bondage, They are the works of Satan and Jesus came to undo these works. Matt. 9:33, 1 Jno. 3:8, etc. The first figure represents the individual under affliction (It could be a hundred and one different ailments); the demons

47

are In operation. The right hand figure shows a person praying very earnestly. Sometimes, these demons relax their hold while praying and are eliminated entirely. Oftentimes, however, the demons relax their hold but are not entirely cast out because of UNBELIEF, consequently they take up their task again and continue in the person (unless a great degree of holding faith Is put into practice). Prayer, combined with fasting, sees the demons not only release and relax their hold, but a greater amount of faith is developed so they can be cast out entirely. Oftentimes, the FAST has such purifying power, both physically and spiritually, that demons are often forced to withdraw.

DEMONS AT WORK IN THE STOMACH. Medical science claims that 95% of the American people are auto-intoxicated (surfeited). Luke 21:34, Most functional diseases come from over eating and the failure to give our stomach a vacation. When sick, the first thing a doctor looks at is the tongue, which is a part of the stomach. A weakened condition of the stomach will attract demons. This could lead to a hundred and one different things. We believe they are demons. It could be ulcer, tumor, cancer, rheumatism, asthma, anemia, hardening of the arteries, paralysis, etc.

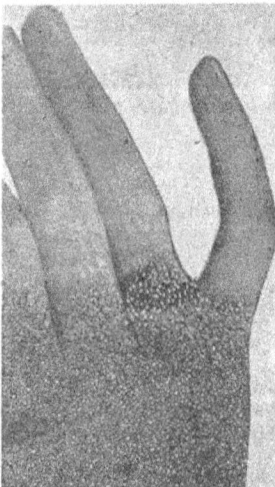

When fasting, the things we do not want make the best of fuel for their own destruction. Body toxins, slowly and gradually, accumulate all through the body in almost every person in time. Sometimes, it shows itself in a visible manner through muddy skin, blemishes, pale complexion or lines and wrinkles. Sometimes, it is not very visible. At the bottom of the hand, we are depicting a condition where waste matter can be visualized under magnification. Demons are more easily attracted through these conditions. One of the first things that takes place in the consecration fast is the removal and eradication of all foreign uncleanness of the body. After only a ten day fast, in most instances, the hand will ap. pear as the fingers appear in the top part of the illustration. A spiritual cleansing of the doubts and our main objective to please Jesus.

Demons and disease breed on filth. The more vile it is the more potent is its lure for all demons, and from this source we have the root of all sickness, disease and sorrow. Demons seldom enter clean healthy people.

In spite of all the food that is eaten, there is truly a famine in the world. There is a famine within the stomach, not because of the absence of food, but because of an excess of food, and because of the failure to FAST and starve out a condition within that is incapable of handling and receiving more food. Why put new wine in old bottles? Why sew new cloth to old?

The failure to eat plain simple food also causes the body to become so depleted from the lack of minerals and vitamins that, even if folk would receive the secondary blessings from fasting, which are physical, they could not retain their new-found health very long if they did not adapt their menu to natural plain eating. Of course, one can take vegetable concentrates, fish oils and food minerals as a supplement. These are not drugs, but are concentrated food in tablet form. These may be helpful, but the better way is to follow Jesus in proper abstemious living.

Why close our ears to it? The very reason that it is not more understood is simply that people are prejudiced and run from the truth, willingly becoming the victims of their own foolishness—just because they fail to earnestly and intelligently seek KNOWLEDGE and TRUTH ON THIS GREAT, BENEFICIAL, FUNDAMENTAL PRINCIPLE OF THE CHRISTIAN RELIGION.

FASTING will give a *PERFECT BLOOD STREAM,* INSURE the *PERFECT DISTRIBUTION OF THE BLOOD* AND THE *CONSERVATION OF ENERGY.* THESE THREE THINGS ARE THE THREE ESSENTIALS vital to any sick person and their desire to get well, and their chances for recovery. Another ESSENTIAL that is a result of consecrated fasting is SPIRITUAL HEALTH.

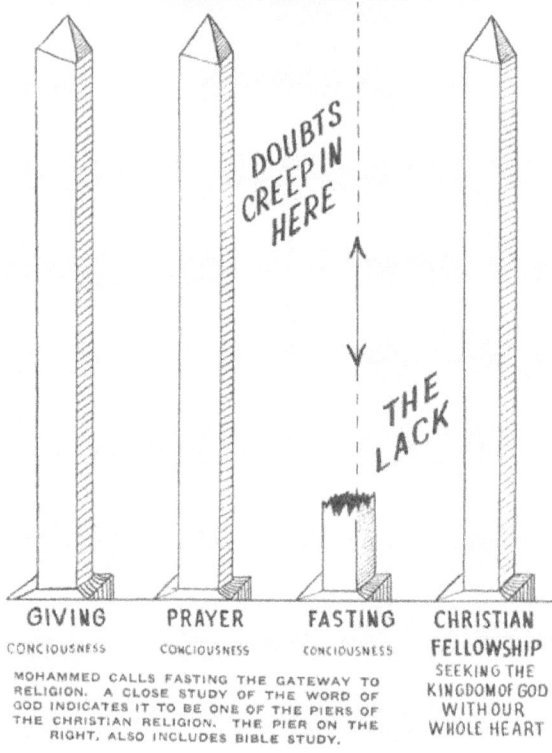

MARK FOR THE PRIZE OF THE HIGH CALLING
PHIL. 3:14 II PET 1:10

DOUBTS CREEP IN HERE

THE LACK

| GIVING | PRAYER | FASTING | CHRISTIAN |
| CONCIOUSNESS | CONCIOUSNESS | CONCIOUSNESS | FELLOWSHIP |

MOHAMMED CALLS FASTING THE GATEWAY TO RELIGION. A CLOSE STUDY OF THE WORD OF GOD INDICATES IT TO BE ONE OF THE PIERS OF THE CHRISTIAN RELIGION. THE PIER ON THE RIGHT, ALSO INCLUDES BIBLE STUDY.

SEEKING THE KINGDOM OF GOD WITH OUR WHOLE HEART

Many are seeking cures today. They are trying to find an easy way to overcome their ailments, when the easiest, surest, quickest and most economical method ever known to man IS THE FAST ROUTE. There are hundreds of millions of dollars spent annually on patent medicines alone. Eighty percent of every dollar spent is for advertising these cure-all pills. Five cents worth of onions has more food value than all the drugs put together.

A government document, No. 264, informs us that ninety-nine percent of the American people are deficient in minerals, and that a marked deficiency in any one of the more important minerals actually results in disease.

Food is the major part of any right living program. Sick people are actually starving amidst an abundance of food, The sick have stomachs filled with foodless food.

WE ARE A PRODUCT OF WHAT WE EAT

Dr. Northen's experiment with animals and soil chemistry has given the world much information. He has discovered when rats are fed the same "refined to death food" found in an over-stuffed community filled with stomach ulcers, the rats likewise have stomach ulcers.

Experiments on rats and mice in Chicago definitely prove that the irritating matter contained in canned foods, preservatives, canned spices and drugs will produce cancer in animals eating such foods. We know, also, that rats fed the diet of the Britisher take on the temperament of the British people. When the Sikh diet is fed rats, they become huge and have soulful eyes, the same as the followers of that Hindu creed.

Human beings are also a product of what they eat. When we live by the "words of God" instead of "bread alone," the spiritual food that is received through fasting makes us more spiritual for the glory of Jesus. The spiritual gifts and fruit are developed in us plus other attributes.

Fasting will also prepare our stomachs for food, so that the digestive organs will be capable of greater absorption of the mineral salts that our body is in need of. When there is over indulgence in food, without fasting, only a smaller amount of the vitamins and minerals can be assimilated, because of the contaminated condition of the stomach and villi.

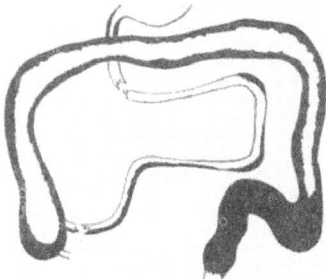

MONTHS-OLD CONTAMINATION

The chart depicts the painted coating of food film which is nothing more than, weeks and sometimes many months old, decayed and rotten contaminated food on the intestinal tract. If this intestinal tract was placed in front of us and was accessible, we would not hesitate to give it a good cleaning. Cleanliness is Godliness, we all admit. Because we cannot see this precious God given organ, we hesitate to go into food abstention to give it a vacation and cleaning. Fasting will eradicate this uncleanness and removes many pounds of demon attracting filth that saps not only physical but spiritual strength from the temple of the Holy Spirit. Fasting consumes the very things

FASTED FORTY DAYS — DEMONS LEAVE BODY

Dear Brother Hall:

About the tenth day of October, 1947, I went into "The Book and Bible House," on Eighth Street, in Sacramento, California, to purchase a song book. I wanted to practice singing so I could glorify Jesus by making a joyful noise unto Him. An employee of the "Bible House" told me of having some very unusual books they had never had on hand before in the history of the firm. This was Sister Delmarie Bibb, and she got them out and showed them to me. Miss Bibb informed me that the truth contained in them was unfolding unheard of precious experiences for people in the days that we live. I did not know what they were all about, but I secured a set of these books on the

PROPHET'S-EARLY CHURCH-LENGTH FASTING.

At this very time, I was so very hungry for more of God, I wanted to go deeper and seek Him in an unusual manner. I began reading and studying these books on consecrated fasting on October 14, the day I started my fast.

I cried and prayed, and the misery of fasting was painful at times, but I knew it would be a battle, and the old man had to be conquered. At times, it seemed I was getting nowhere, and I felt I was not praying as earnestly as I should. Although it was hard to pray, I just did my best and trusted Jesus to take me through. It was so discouraging, but when the Fourteenth day of the fast came around I found new encouragement. The asthma that I had had for eight years left my body completely, and demons left along with it. I actually could see these demons in every corner of my room. I even saw them come out of my body. From then on I felt like a NEW MAN. Before the fast, I never in my life saw a demon and I never even knew they occupied my body until this very time. When these demons came out, other parts of my afflicted body became well, healed and whole.

For twenty years I had suffered with crooked bent-under toes. When the demons left my body, the toes straightened upwards and they pained me. They went out and upwards for two days. I suffered very severely, but I was sure they were getting healed and sure enough they were. The pains were from the straightening out process that was necessary in order for them to become adjusted to the right position, etc. Because I cried and prayed to Jesus about this, He relieved me from all the pains of the healing procedure. I then cried and wept for joy at the miracle He had done in my body by casting out these demons -- He said in His word they would be cast out, sometimes "by nothing, BUT BY PRAYER AND FASTING." Matt. 17:21. My toes and feet were made perfectly whole and sound. I had been praying for a long time that this might be done, but, praise Jesus, it took fasting with the prayer.

I also had a great need for my own place to live. I needed a home but could not find a place. Again I became somewhat discouraged. Considerable weight was lost from my body. When the fast was started, I weighed two hundred four pounds. There was a scale nearby and as I got on to weigh, a friend came up. I weighed one hundred sixty pounds. This friend seeing my baggy clothes, asked me, 'What's wrong, you look like you have been sick, or something has come over you all of a sudden.' I told him 'I was not sick, hut Saturday would be the end of my forty-day fast and I was somewhat disappointed, for it seemed I would not get all that I wanted and was fasting for! He asked rue 'what I wanted,' and I told him "I would like to have a house trailer for a place to call home and live in.' He informed me 'that my prayer was answered and he had just what I had been looking for. When I went over to see it, I was delighted to know it was the answer to my prayer, because it was just what I wanted, Not only did I get the house trailer at a fraction of the cost, but I was given over one hundred dollars worth of groceries, a radio, two stoves, electric plate, clock, furnishings, etc.

On January 26, 1948, I will be sixty-five years old. I feel wonderful in my body. It seems like I have gained about twenty-five years of youth for my body.

I attend The Full Gospel Lighthouse Church where Brother Leroy Richardson is pastor, in North Sacramento, Calif. They will verify these facts,

This brought such great joy to my soul that I went home and prayed all night asking the Lord to unfold this fasting message to others, and I prayed that others would know about this testimony so they, too, would see the answers to their hitherto unanswered prayers, like I had received. I prayed, if it be His will, this testimony would go into Brother Hall's new book, "GLORIFIED FASTING," that will be full of testimonies about fastings of all lengths.

Your Brother in Christ,

(Signed) Thomas H. Lymons

Box 386, Yolo, Calif.

FASTING PRODUCES OIL OF THE SPIRIT

FASTING POWER: Fasting produces the greater oil that gives us the spiritual fire of the Holy Spirit. It digs down into the spiritual OIL WELL, and there is plenty of fuel for revival power in us, to spread and spring forth out of us, to ignite lost souls to Christ and help spread the revival fires to others. Prayer is also an oil producer, but too many of us depend on prayer altogether without fastings and, consequently, we get stuck at times. Fasting is as necessary in the Christian's life as oxygen is to keep the fire going. A fire will burn a long time in an air tight room, but, sooner or later, the oxygen will be used up and the flame will go out. A person may get along nicely for a very long time without fastings, but, sooner or later, carnality creeps in and, unconsciously, the child of God thinks he is standing when he should take heed lest he has fallen.

"Without faith it is impossible to please God." We have seen, according to the seventeenth chapter of Matthew, fasting and prayer is the great faith producer. The left hand person has sufficient oil and fire in his lamp. He is laboring for Jesus in the harvest fields. We believe he is fasting and praying a great deal The middle person has both oil and some fire, but he is indifferent to fasting, therefore, there are very few signs following and very little accomplished for Jesus. The right individual is typical of the five foolish virgins (Matt. 25:18) who were NOT WATCHING. "Watching," in these scriptures, include everything necessary for the Bride of Christ to be doing, ready and filled with the spirit. This includes fasting and prayer. When this lamp is suddenly moved or trimmed it may go out. May we have more oil.

THE BREAK FAST

The word, BREAK-FAST, is used over and over by nearly every one, without realizing exactly what it means. A long time ago, people were not in the habit of eating between meals, and were not able to go to the corner drug store, or restaurant, and buy a soda, sandwich, cup of coffee and what not as easily as one can do in our own time. Our great grandfathers worked hard and had healthy appetites. When a hearty evening meal was eaten, they usually ceased eating for a long interval, at least, from the evening meal until the following morning. This interval was the longest period between any two meals. It being so long that sometimes it was called a "FAST." Please see, Daniel 6: 18. "The King . . . passed the night fasting." If any food was eaten after the evening meal, it proceeded to break the period between the evening meal and the morning meal and was breaking the fast. In the morning, when food was eaten again, it could not very well be called a break-fast, because the fast period between the evening and morning meals had been broken already.

Break-fast is a compound word that usage has welded into breakfast. At breakfast, one usually eats a meal that is different from the other two eaten during the day. (I am alluding to those who eat breakfast. Many adults are finding they have better health and greater spiritual power without eating breakfast. This also includes the author who has not eaten breakfast in twenty-four years.) The interval between dinner and breakfast being long enough that folk have found it both desirable and wise to partake of food at the morning meal that is far more acceptable to the stomach and digestive apparatus than that eaten at any other meal. The reason for this is quite evident; it is to prepare the stomach and functions of the body to break the fast, even though one has only done without food for approximately twelve to fourteen hours. Even this short a fast, if one may still call it that, is usually broken with care, however unaware the average person is of the fact. The breakfast eater usually has a glass of fruit juice or similar juice, eggs, bacon and toast or cereal, etc. This menu, compared with any other conventional meal, is far more easily digested and more suitable to the break-fast period than any other of his or her eating periods. It may not have been thought of in this light, but the fast was carefully broken for just that non-eating length of time.

If any adult who was not undernourished, and some undernourished folk would also profit by it, would leave off any one of the three meals for a period of thirty days, the third meal habit appetite would entirely disappear and new energy and strength would be felt, in addition to greatly increased spiritual power and favor with God. Why? Because the average person does not in any manner require this surplus third meal. While any one meal could be left out, the author feels that greater compensation would be obtained by leaving off the breakfast—or allowing the lunch period to be the breakfast. This longer interval between the eating of dinner and breakfast (or lunch) would give the organs of the body a greater period in which to relax and rest up, and also the appetite would, generally, more easily adapt itself to the new schedule. As one grows older, even less food is required. Sometimes one could eliminate the second meal also and not be bothered with habit hunger appetite, after abstaining from two meals a day for at least thirty days. This is one secret to long life. Why? For the simple reason, what one does not need becomes burdensome and a dead weight to us.

Paul must have had this also in mind in Hebrews 12:1: "Lay aside every weight, and the sin which doth so easily beset us, and let us run with patience the race that is set before us." At least, the continued eating and stuffing habit, without fasting, becomes weight (not necessarily physical weight) and a hindrance to our spiritual progress. Paul brings this out to a fuller extent in Romans 16:17, 18: "Mark them which cause divisions and offences contrary to the doctrine which ye have learned; and AVOID THEM. For they that are such serve not our Lord Jesus Christ, but their own belly." Also, study Phil. 3:17-19. Please see charts on subject.

I have a car that runs well, but many times I load it up with books and tracts—taking even the rear cushions out to pile in some more until I have nearly two thousand pounds of material to carry from one town to another to be used in speaking engagements where hungry folk desire and need the literature and books. The car, being overloaded, does not run so freely; it is more difficult to keep on the road, the tires become overheated to a point where I am forced to slow down to keep from having a blow-out. (By failing to drive around forty miles an hour with these loads, the author has had three new six ply heavy duty tires to blow-out in one year, due to this excess weight.) This

burdensome weight is eventually needed and can all be utilized, but many handicaps hindered me during my travels. After learning some expensive lessons, I corrected the weight and I have since progressed very satisfactorily. The same lesson can also be applied to food power versus needed power. Any excess of food not needed now, will burn out the body prematurely, and act as a weight and a hindrance to it. Excess food will kill spiritual power just as thoroughly as alcohol will, if not as quickly. (See Luke 21:34. Food temperance is just as important as any other kind of temperance. Many times, unknowingly, we are killing our bodies and souls, just because of our neglect along these lines.

THE WEIGHT GROOVE

No matter how long an individual fasts, it may be either a short or long fast, the person breaking a fast will become hungry. His hunger may become very intense, even though he broke the fast before the real return of hunger. There usually develops an intensity of hunger that is nothing short of a desire for alcohol. This extreme return of the desire of hunger is for a period of approximately only three days. No matter what one eats.

or how much he may eat, he will still be very hungry. He cannot become satisfied; and right here is the danger and most critical point of the entire fast and the breaking in period. At the end of forty days and forty nights of fasting, Jesus Christ, our Lord, had hunger to return at its intensity. His temptation was at this critical moment, but He overcame the Devil and also overcame His appetites. If the fasting candidate wishes to obtain all that he should from the fast, it is right at this point, the point of breaking the fast properly and carefully. These first three days are the most important whether he fast for three days, twenty-one days or for forty-days, the victories that one will have forever afterwards are determined largely how he or she overcomes the appetites after the initial breaking-in period.

If one is overweight and wishes to continue along the line of weight that he lost during the fast, then these first few days, at least the first three days must be so very carefully broken. After three days, the appetite becomes so adjusted to receiving small amounts of food that hunger does not bother one too much thereafter, unless one g or ges and stimulates the appetite abnormally. By being careful, one can retain his proper weight.

A weight groove is formed in the stomach so weight will not be regained easily. If underweight, one can also gain healthy additional pounds, when the fast is properly and slowly broken. (See author's volume "Because of Your Unbelief" on weight).

Brother Hall you may be surprised to as given in your book, and with FAITH, learn how God healed me of T.B. upon a BIG Faith, the Lord completely reading your wonderful book entitled, healed me!

"BECAUSE OF YOUR UNBELIEF".. So, when I heard of your coming to this was back in 1953. By strictly the Philippines, I was very thrilled. following your instructions on fasting Mrs. E. Sebastian

tomatoes, berries or easily digested melons in moderate quantity. Second day: Same.

Succeeding days: For third day here, follow the second day schedule under the breaking of a three to six day fast, and continue.

After a fast of ten to fourteen days— First two days: After the break-fast on any FRESH fruit juice, at the next meal

eat CHOICE FRESH CITRUS FRUIT moderately. For the balance of the two days, eat three or four meals of fresh citrus fruit only, each meal four and one-half hours or more apart and consisting of 6 to 8 ounces.

Third day: Light soups or skimmed, whole, or buttermilk at each meal time. Fourth day: Green salads or cooked light vegetables chewed to milk.

Protein foods such as nuts, cottage cheese, cheese products, eggs, lentiles etc. should be eaten in proper quantities, when fast is broken properly.

Fifth day and after: Three meals protein fruits and vegetables fruit or milk (or buttermilk). Buttermilk is easier to digest than sweet milk. (The over use of milk or the taking of food too soon may cause the body to bloat slightly. To remedy this cut down the quantity or wait a few days before going on the milk diet.) If one should bloat, fast and go without water. Take enemas and hot baths.

After a fast of two weeks to twenty-one days— First day: Three meals of fruit juice in four to six ounce serving, diluted one-

third to one-half with water.

Second day: Three or four meals of same, somewhat less diluted, in servings of from six to eight ounces.

Third day: Fruit for each meal.

Fourth day: Duplicate third day, or a half pint of milk or buttermilk every two or three hours, or eat choice of one light soup, a small fruit or green vegetable salad at meal times.

Fifth day: three light meals 'spaced properly apart, either fresh fruit or soup. Always get plenty of rest.

Succeeding days: Very gradually work up from fruit, milk, and soup to vegetable meals. Eat slowly and chew everything into milk.

Suggestions for sixth or seventh day: Noon—Vegetables and whole wheat cereal with one or two egg yolks if desired. Evening—Similar meal without eggs.

After a fast of twenty-one to forty days or longer— The same program is followed as for a fourteen to twenty-one day fast, except smaller amounts of food are eaten for the first two or three days. Add one or two more days of fruit juices before beginning fourth day, described just. above. Orange juice, is the preferred juice, though any natural fresh fruit juice or fruit, tomato, gruel, barley rice water, ripe watermelon, or clear vegetable broth may be taken, in four to six ounce servings. The quantity may be increased when prepared for heavier diet. Warm milk may be added to the water-made cereal preparations later on after the fast is broken properly.

Fruit and milk are far preferable to other types of food, since they are Peering Into the Wonderful Digestive Mechanism.

The intestinal canal is crowded with five million finger-like "VILLI." Each villus does its small part In the digestion process and contains three thousand cells each. This would make fifteen billion cells in the Intestinal wall that are very much alive and ready to act when brought into contact with food. After fasting they can receive only minute particles of food nourishment at first. Among the cells, one finds single goblet cells that produce mucus. Phagocytes wander out of the lymph nodes and participate in transporting food particles. (See bottom of diagram). When a protracted fast is broken, these cells gradually and very slowly become reawakened from a deep sleep. The sleep is so sound that only a few thousand of these cells are awakened when the first juice contacts the villi after a major fast. A first layer of these cells begin to yawn and come into activity. A few hours later another "break-fast" menu Is taken, a few more thousand, and even the villi, this time, come out of their dormant condition to receive food, convert it Into nourishment, and push It into the blood. Each time another installment of the proper "break-fast" menu Is received, the villi Increase and increase into activity and receptivity until eventually, after a number of days, the entire intestinal canal is fully activated and adjusted to food again for our blessing.

natural foods and more likely to be digested and assimilated perfectly, and to perpetuate without interruption the physical results secured by the fast.

Remember, if you should suffer in any way, even though it should be many days after the fast, it is because you are rushing the breaking in period. The remedy is to go back to fruit juices, or fast again. Two meals may be more preferable to three, for a while anyway.

The wonderful finger-like structure of the digestive apparatus, gradually and slowly reawakens. It yawns and stretches, so to speak, as it first becomes reacquainted with food. Impairment and shock, through the over-use of food, will abuse this marvelous organ so that it cannot be the blessing that it was intended to be. Fasting proves itself to be one of the best blessings from the Lord for this vital organ.

THE REVIVAL OF THE INTESTINAL APPARATUS

The diet God gave to Adam in his perfect state, before the fall is the best type of a diet for the born again, restored to God through the second Adam, Jesus Christ, today. These were fruits and vegetables (Gen. 1:29). "Herbs," here, are vegetables. Nuts, cheese and the whole seed foods (grain lentiles etc.) are good body builders after the fast.

All of these fifteen billion cells that comprise five million villi fingers (medical statistics) in the complicated digestive system, have to be reawakened little by little after a protracted fast. Certain stages of the BREAK-FAST PERIOD may represent a certain proportion of these cells and fingers coming out of a slumber and waking up for breakfast.

These villi.fingers may be compared to a person's hand or foot going to sleep for a long time. We cannot awaken the foot or hand immediately. But, little by little, one feels the tingle or sensation of awakening until it gradually, but with increasing tempo, becomes restored to normal.

The tiny fingers of the digestive system secrets juices that help to dissolve food into nutriment. These hair-like fingers likewise become, though very slowly at first, awakened and adjusted to food reception again after the breakfast. At first, they very, very slowly become reaccustomed to food intake, but the acceleration is more and more rapid, until the digestive canal is back into full swing again. Not only restored to the condition that it was in at the beginning of food abstention, but the entire intestinal tubing has had a complete revival and is now like new.

• The author is, herewith, presenting an estimate of the reawakening in the digestive system, period by period, of the five million villi fingers that make up the converter when breaking fast. We are using a twenty-one day fast for a yardstick; for a longer or shorter fast, one can make estimates from this schedule.

The approximate number of villi fingers that are re-awakened after breaking a twenty-one day fast, and that are slowly acclimated to food again are:

WHY THE FAST MUST BE BROKEN CAREFULLY

First   twenty-four hours: 12,500 villi. (Approximately one-fourth of one percent).

Second day: 25,000 fingers (About one-half of one percent).

Third day: 50,000 villi fingers (About one percent).

Fourth day: 100,000 villi (Two percent).

Fifth day: 200,000 villi (Four percent).

Sixth day: 400,000 villi (Eight percent).

Seventh day: 800,000 villi (Sixteen percent).

Eighth day: 1,600,000 villi (Thirty-two percent).

Ninth day: 2,400,000 villi (About forty-eight percent). Please note from this time on, the percentage begins to drop. The breaking-in to the eating process tapers back the other way from the eighth day onward. A person usually begins to feel a newness of strength and well-being from this time onward. (Providing the fast is being broken properly.)

Tenth day: 3,000,000 villi.

Eleventh day: 3,600,000 villi. Twelfth day: 4,000,000 villi,

There is still another 1,000,000 to yet be divided. This may be

distributed over a period of from one to two weeks (or even longer in some cases) before they become fully awakened.

The purpose of this part of our study is to reveal more vividly to the reader that our digestive apparatus is far more complicated than is generally thought, and needs as much respect for its delicate and intricate nature as any other part of the body for the Glory of Jesus. Let us give Jesus glory in our body, in our soul, and in our spirit. If our stomach is part of us, why not let it also glorify Him who also redeemed it. In the last chapter of Revelation, when we eat the new food from the new tree of life, we will then have our new redeemed stomach to enjoy to the utmost this delicious food.

ENGLISH BROTHER TRIES FAST AND HAS BETTER OUTLOOK

Dear Brother in Christ:

I was glad to receive the books and pamphlets, which I have distributed among my Christian friends, and I am especially delighted with the book, "Atomic Power with God Thru Fasting and Prayer." This is just what we lack in England. As soon as I received the book I started on a fast. Although I work long hours every day, I feel so much better and my asthma is almost gone. I have suffered terribly and have been prayed for, many times I was at my wit's end. Now, praise the Lord, I have the solution and there is no fear of fasting any more. Jesus has given me a brighter outlook. I am so happy and thrilled over what Jesus is doing for me through fasting and prayer. Soon I expect to send you a testimony of a much longer fast than this one.

Yours in Christ,

John Martin

39 Leek Road, Weston Coyney

Stoke-on-Trent, Staffs, England.

NINE LAYERS OF THE INTESTINE

In order that the reader may be more appreciative and thankful to Jesus for one of the most magic-like organs in his body, we are, herewith, presenting a section of the "INTESTINAL MUCOUS MEMBRANE" for your observation. The intestinal wall is not much thicker than a page of paper in this volume, but yet possess a most ingenious

structure, there are no less than nine layers (1-9) that make up this life producing structure. The uppermost, inner layer consists of high columnar cells. The exposed ends of these cells exhibit a bright striated edge which is probably of great significance in the absorption of the digested food. Among these cells are others, shaped like goblets and filled with a special protoplasmatic product called mucin. In the upper left corner a goblet cell is shown in the act of pouring out its contents: in the opposite corner an empty goblet cell is seen in the resting stage. Goblet cells are the smallest glands in the body. When fasting, these cells and layers are also renovated, purified and cleansed. This is one of the key points to which demons can become attracted to an individual. Many times they attack and leave. This may go on for many months or even years. Then a weakened condition results from millions of cells and villi becoming contaminated through our "surfeiting" habits (Luke 21 :34, also see Psalm 78) and failure to fast, and demons gain foothold and an ulcer, cancer, tumor or some other disease that may, or may not, bear a fancy name, will develop. Our digestive tract is one of the most important and mysterious organs of the temple of the Holy Ghost. Let us protect it and give it proper vacations for the Glory of Jesus.

JESUS HAS GIVEN US FASTING FOR CLEAN LIVING

AND FAITH LIVING

If it is not the will of God for us to be healed today, then every doctor and hospital is a reproach to the cause of Christ, They would be counter to the will of Jesus. If it isn't the Lord's will to heal us today—why go to doctors, why take medicine, why go to a hospital and try to get well? When did the Lord provide a less successful method to heal the sick than the method of FAITH HEALING than He used in His day? Jesus is no respecter of persons.

If He healed people in His day in answer to FAITH, He surely wants to heal members of His body today. He, surely, does not want a diseased body.

The Literary Digest contained the statement that there were thirty thousand doctors too many in the United States. (The inefficient, undesirable doctors).

I cannot believe that Jesus wants doctors, hospitals and drugs to take the place of DIVINE HEALING TODAY. Efficient doctors and hospitals have their place and can be a blessing to people who do not have Jesus to lean upon. It is a disgrace, however, to the medical profession that, with the number of doctors we have, there are so many sick people. Surely, there must be something wrong. How many people are told what brought on their partciular ailment? How many sick people are taught how to live clean lives, and how to prevent disease? How many diseased folk are told that FOOD ABSTENTION is the GREATEST NATURAL CURATIVE AGENCY KNOWN TO MAN? We might ask a question of these doctors. How much do you know about Jesus Christ's plain simple method of clean living through FASTING?

Both cancer and diabetes are on the increase. "One out of eight persons will die of cancer this year," states a government report. Fasting and right Christian living will ward off and prevent these two ailments alone. Jesus can and will heal them if present, WHEN UNBELIEF is not present.

METHODIST PASTOR FASTS FORTY DAYS—MIGHTY REVIVAL

Dear Brother Hall:

Praise the Lord, I was by His help able to carry through the forty-day and night fast, (only water taken). I am fifty-four and lost forty-five pounds. At the beginning I weighed two hundred-ten pounds. I came down to one hundred sixty-five.

I had some bilious trouble along with an ether-like taste, otherwise, I got along nicely. I would say it was a most glorious experience, perhaps, the greatest in my whole life.

I feel somehow that fasting for the glory of our Lord is the answer to many of our problems; it will also bring the glorious success to revival campaigns.

I am glad to say that we are NOW IN THE MIDST OF A MIGHTY CITY-WIDE REVIVAL—with Mr. Harper and Mr. Long, Christian business men of Iowa.

Spiritually, I am much stronger, but, even at that, I always feel that I need much more of the 'POWER OF CHRIST in my life.

This is my eighteenth day of the breaking-in period and I have been eating soups and vegetables. I have regained about fifteen pounds. My ankles are swollen a little bit but not noticeably.

I would like to know if it might be possible for your evangelistic party to come to Clinton, maybe some time next summer for a Revival? . .

Oh yes, I have both of your books, 'Atomic Power With God' and 'The Fasting Prayer.' They are very good.

Sincerely in the Master's service,

J.   Howard Machlan, pastor of "The Methodist Church" Clinton, Iowa.

LADY'S BROTHER DRUNKARD FOR THIRTY YEARS

DELIVERED FOR GOOD AFTER TWELVE DAYS FASTING

Dear Brother in Christ:

I PRAYED FOR MY 'DRUNKARD BROTHER FOR EIGHT YEARS WITH SEEMINGLY NO RESULTS. THEN I GOT DESPERATE ABOUT HIS DELIVERANCE and fasted to Jesus for twelve days. On the second day of the fast I got sick and ate some rice. It seemed to help me and I continued the fast ten days more, making a total of twelve days. I drank distilled water which tasted much better than the city water. I felt weak at times and prayed this prayer: "I can do all things in Christ Jesus who strengtheneth me. Greater is He that is in me than he that is in the world."

I did all my housework and was surprised that one could go on, as I am twenty-five pounds underweight. I am five feet six inches tall, weigh one hundred pounds, fifty-nine years old and feel like twenty-five young in the Spirit.

Just thirty days after I broke the fast my sister-in-law wrote a letter to me telling that my brother was completely delivered from drink with no desire or temptation to drink any more—and is serving the Lord.

It is now six months later and he is still free from the drinking demon. He was a drunkard for thirty years.

There is pleasure in fasting, knowing that our prayers will be answered.

I have other relatives that I intend going into another fast for, so I can see them also converted.

The fast was broken too rapidly and my mouth became sore. Next time I will eat more wisely.

In Him whom we love,

Mary C. Wilkie Pasadena   Calif.

EVANGELIST JOE WILKES

By these Holy Ghost fasts lean now speak the word of faith. I need not pray the old long prayers that I used to. I get great results with short prayers. When I command the sick to get healed, they just get healed. Sickness, pains and demons move when I speak it in Jesus dear name. The gift of faith really works by fasting. The Lord enables me to put or impart the Holy Ghost Fire upon the people that want the Holy Ghost Baptism fully.

I sat under the teachings of Rev. Velma Sanders and also received help. I know I must also support this ministry with my offerings. It is a ministry that is doing so much more for others. It goes beyond the salvation in the heart, It brings salvation upon the body.

In your 1971 convention in Phoenix I was also greatly blessed and appreciated the work more than ever. I enjoy your books and Miracle Word Magazine.

In Christ,

Evangelist Joe Wilkes, Chicago, Ill.

Delivered From Nicotine—12 Loved Ones Saved

Dear Brother Hall,

My husband received your books in the mail while I was at mothers for the week. He was exuberant telling me about them, for we know what power there is in

fasting along with your praying. We know God is a prayer answering God when everything is done by the "Book."

Our lives and home have been completely renovated by the coming in of Christ, whom we so badly neglected for forty years. We've made Christ the head of our house and now all the wrinkles are smoothed out and we live in peace, harmony and love.

God has healed me of migraine and sinus headaches, and also my fifteen year old son of deteriorating retina that would have blinded him completely by age 25. Oh! Praise His Wonderful name. It will be a year tomorrow that God took the nicotine habit from us, we had smoked 27 years. We acceptedGod'sgift of salvation just a year ago. We believe that your way (fasting) is Christ's way, for we have seen twelve of our loved ones saved in the past year. The power of fasting and prayer surely helped us.

Please send your magazine. Here are names to send tracts to. God Bless you and Sister Hall.

Your sister in Christ,

Mrs. R. D. Heeth, Grand Prairie, Texas.

One of the five million Gastric Glands contained in the mucous membrane of the stomach, which secrete pepsin, rennin, and hydrochloric acid juice.

The Gastric Glands are another reason why a protracted fast must be broken slowly and carefully. These five million glands in the wall of the stomach are very industrious. When eating, they produce three quarts of secretion daily.

THE MEDICINE MAN

In South America, the wild savage has his tribal medicine man or witch doctor. In order to become a medicine man, he has to live for weeks without food, and then chews bark, roots and plants. He also has to go through a ritual of weird and wild maneuvers before obtaining this high position in the spirit realm. He is supposed to control warfare, crop failures, floods and nearly everything else, and is also supposed to have great influence with the spirit world. If through fasting, a savage is made almost a God in his tribe, how much more ought Christians to fast to have special favor and power with their God?

'For as in the days that were before the flood they were eating and drinking." Mart. 24:39. The "DRINKING" in this reference included FOOD and beverage drinks as well as alcoholic drinks. There is not a bit of harm in eating and drinking good food, but there is plenty of harm to the Christian's spirituality when the eating and drinking habit is continued without fasting. In Luke 21:34, we are told the same thing in stronger language. The "OVERCHARGED WITH SURFEITING" condition that shall be prevalent in these days might sound like this in every day language. Stop! look! listen! My coming will be in the midst of both food and drink and other drunkenness. It is possible for you to be so wrapped up with the cares of these pleasures that My coming will be overlooked and you will not be ready.

As soon as we let loose of food, and all of the cares connected with our customary "MUCH SERVINGS" (See Luke 10:4042), we become, immediately, free of many natural burdens and encumbrances, and then our greater attention is given to Jesus.

In food abstention, a release gets underway and our previously engaged blood and energy is released from the laborious task of pushing food through thirty feet of tubing, digesting, assimilating and eliminating. A conservation of energy takes place, but some of this released energy goes to work housecleaning the temple of the Holy Spirit. The blood, not being so occupied taking on more food and garbage, goes out to pick up (even like a person who takes a rake and cleans up the yard) all the poisons within every part of the body where DEMONS harbor. The blood returns heavily laden with toxin and filth like a sewer stream. These very things we do not want are used for energy and while some of it is emptied into the stomach and colon. A bonfire is started (1). The noncombustible residues are eliminated as ashes of faeces (4). This, usually, causes constipation. A clinker is sometimes formed that aggravates constipation during and right after fasting (see No. 4). About twenty-five percent is lost in this manner. Another twenty-five percent is lost in the lungs through the return of the blood (2,3), and out into the nostrils* (one reason for the faster's foul breath), another

twenty-five percent is lost through the skin, and the other twenty-five percent is lost through the kidneys. The "BONFIRE" exudes poisons from the nostrils,

*   A tiny menthol crystal is a satisfactory deodorant for the breath when fasting.

FASTING TWELVE DAYS — SINNERS CONVERTED TO JESUS

Dear Brother Hall:

Your tracts received proved to be most interesting upon the subject of fasting. They helped me to fast twelve days. What a deception Satan uses, holding so many of us under. I can testify that one is helped physically, rather than harmed while fasting.

My faith increased—I have victory over self, flesh and the devil. The Lord rewarded me by giving me souls, and backsliders came back to Him after the fast. Please send some more literature that I can give to my Christian friends and use to help enlighten others to the bigger fasts.

May the Lord bless you in your work for Him. Mary C. Wilkie

Pasadena, Calif.

THE FOCUSING OF ATTENTION ON JESUS

Fasting relaxes the five senses and the consciousness of the environment. The new focus of concentration blazes right through to Jesus.

eAs they ministered to the Lord, and fasted, the

HOLY GHOST SAiD,"

Acts 13:2

Historical developments were in the making. The church at Antioch in Syria was waiting on God and fasting when the Holy Ghost spoke. This is called the FIRST missionary journey in the first church. The Holy Ghost will always speak to us when we wait on Him in fastings. Many times our attentions are so taken up that it is impossible to hear the Holy Ghost when He wants to speak. Fasting enables us to set free the natural, it prevents the flesh from going into a raid and puts the Holy Spirit to work. One can have the Holy Spirit without having the full power

and operation of Him manifested in our lives.

Please note: "The Holy Ghost SAID." If we are not close enough to the Holy Ghost, then there is "FASTING" to help us become adjusted to the spiritual environment.

Again there was more fasting and prayer: "And when they had fasted and prayed." Acts 13:3. A revival began and Jesus was preached.

A. FAMINE WITH FOOD

69

With stomachs packed, people are still in famine. Yes, a famine in days of plenty. Here is the scripture:

BEHOLD THE DAYS COME

(Saith the Lord God)

I WILL SEND A FAMINE IN THE LAND

NOT A FAMINE OF BREAD NOR A THIRST FOR WATER

BUT OF HEARING THE WORDS OF THE LORD

Amos 8:11

This scripture clearly indicates the trend of the very day we live in, In prophecy, nearly three thousand years ago, Amos predicted a condition that would be prevailing where the Lord's people would have plenty of food, but the lack of spiritual bread of the words of the Lord would result in famine. The condition, of course, is the failure of the Lord's people to seek Him in Fasting and Prayer. When gluttony is an ever present habit, we lose sight of the spiritual and become unknowingly famished for same.

"Of hearing the words of the Lord." We can not HEAR the words of the Lord when we are satiated and gross from continually stuffing ourselves. This therefore leads us into a most deplorable state of affairs.

In behalf of a world-wide revival, before it will be too late, we ask the reader to join with thousands of others in fasting and prayer, NOW!

Please send in names and addresses of Christians and we will mail free literature on subject.

www.ingramcontent.com/pod-product-compliance
Lightning Source LLC
Chambersburg PA
CBHW041927260326
41914CB00009B/1204